Humanomics

HOW WE CAN MAKE
THE ECONOMY SERVE US
—NOT DESTROY US

HUMANOMICS

HOW WE CAN MAKE
THE ECONOMY SERVE US
—NOT DESTROY US

EUGEN LOEBL

RANDOM HOUSE • NEW YORK

FOR GRETA

CONTENTS

Humanomics

HOW WE CAN MAKE
THE ECONOMY SERVE US
—NOT DESTROY US

FOREWORD

For a number of years now, economists have questioned the relevance of economics. Now a new question is being asked: Is "economics" actually responsible for the crisis with which mature economies are burdened?

In my view, and this is the departure point of this study, economics *is* responsible for our deepening crisis. I am convinced that we will not be able to solve our basic problems unless we build a science of economy which enables us to navigate our "spaceship earth" toward humane ends: a "humanomics." Despite the honest criticism many economists address to economics, their criticism is directed at existing theories, assuming that more refined and highly sophisticated theories will solve at least some of our problems. This I believe to be a tragic error.

Conventional economics has become, despite its remarkable degree of sophistication, not only a useless tool, but a dangerous one. Its deceptive application has created a crisis which threatens the very foundations of our civilization.

I am witnessing such a crisis for the second time in my life. Nearly half a century ago, the very foundations of Western Europe were shattered. Democracy had to be salvaged by forces outside of the Continent. The cause of the crisis can be attributed to the fact that while the social systems of Western Europe offered their citizens political rights, they did not in any way respond to the democratic will of the people in the realm of the economy.

During those years, I was studying at the University for World Trade in Vienna. Although economics was the most important subject, none of the theories being taught had any relevance to the real issues, and one could not even find an attempt to cope with any of the most burning problems. The conventional economics of that time offered no goal to fight for.

So long as I remained in Czechoslovakia, my home, I was not exposed to fascism and merely continued to express my "petty-bourgeois" dreams of a harmonious world. Just a few miles from my hometown of Slovakia, however, on the academic grounds in the Vienna I cherished, I was faced with the most brutal and inhumane demonstrations by fanatic Nazis. These confrontations destroyed my illusions and made me realize that to remain in touch with the reality of the situation, I could no longer be neutral and would have to join the fight against Nazism.

At the university, I was educated in the economics of the Austrian marginal utility school, but discovered its irrelevance when faced with the Depression. Discussions with my university friends, especially with the most militant and intellectually best-armed students, the Marxists, led me to study Karl Marx. I was most fascinated with his concept of determinism. His belief that capitalism would end and socialism emerge through a natural process because of historical necessity was a tremendous source of encouragement to me, particularly because Nazism's impact was growing and

Marx's contentions would mean the inevitable defeat of those powerful reactionary forces. I observed the great extent to which big business supported fascism, the vast accumulation of wealth, the great concentration of powers, and the growing poverty of the working class and the poor. To me, all these factors proved the validity of Marx's analysis.

Initially, my acceptance of the Marxist world view arose out of a rational and intellectual impulse, the more so as it suited both my concern for the underprivileged as well as my fear of fascism. However intellectual these motivations were at first, Marxism came to have an emotional impact on me. It absorbed my personal life and became a kind of religious belief. I felt myself to be a member of an "army of the just" and viewed all those who did not follow my faith as "sinners."

When Hitler occupied Czechoslovakia, I took refuge in Great Britain. I found the working class there, relative to that of my native country, rather well-off and devoted to their nation. I admired their heroic stand during the war. But I merely registered these events; I did not allow them to penetrate my world view. I continued to believe in the Marxist theory of class concept despite the thousands of facts proving just the opposite.

The same self-righteous attitude occurred in my visits to America during the war. In Great Britain I joined the Czechoslovak government in exile as head of the Ministry for Economic Reconstruction. In this capacity I was also the representative to UNRRA (the United Nations Relief and Rehabilitation Administration). While in the United States for those agency meetings I was deeply impressed with the standard of living of the workers and the miracles that capitalistic America had achieved in the war industry. America's unconditional aid through UNRRA did not at all fit into my understanding of the concept of capitalism. Still, this experience, so contradictory to what Marxism had taught me to expect, did not touch or affect my thoughts and ideas.

In Czechoslovakia's preparation for postwar reconstruction, political parties found a united front in agreeing on the new structure of the economy. We called it the "Czechoslovak Way to Socialism," a structure based on socialism as well as on our own democratic tradition. Although we regarded the Soviet Union as our closest and best friend, the consensus was not to follow the Soviet model.

While we were intent upon building a new type of democracy and socialism, however, the East-West polarization growing out of the cold war did not stop at the borders of Czechoslovakia. The cold war atmosphere encouraged a climate of confrontation: the Communist party and the left wing of the Social Democrats on the one side, the remaining democratic parties on the other. The far better organized and more militant Communist party easily won this battle, and brought with it a heated period of persecution of "class enemies."

Prior to these events I had spent a few months in the Soviet Union while negotiating a trade agreement. I became acquainted with life there—its economy and planning, its fantastic shortcomings, its many dehumanizing phenomena. All that I disliked I simply declared a deviation, the consequences of the war. In my negotiations in Moscow, Mikoyan, the Soviet Minister of Foreign Trade and a Politburo member, insisted that we trade exclusively with the Soviet Union and to break off the commercial relations with the West that we had been maintaining since the end of the war. I refused these demands, insisting that we had to pursue our own interests. At that time, I was not aware that what I was actually facing was an attempt to deprive my country of any kind of independence.

As a result of this conflict, I was imprisoned in 1949.*

* A detailed account of my prison experiences will be published in the fall of 1976 by Harcourt Brace Jovanovich.

My Soviet interrogators bluntly told me that my negotiations with Mikoyan had proven me an enemy of socialism. I was accused of having acted as a traitor and of attempting to create normal and friendly economic relations with the French, the British, and particularly with the Americans despite the existence of the cold war. Even with this brutal experience, I regarded this form of Soviet imperialism as a "deviation." The idea that my world view was wrong, that I had actually been devoting my life to an unworthy cause was too abhorrent and unacceptable.

The path that had brought me to Marxism—the intellectual avenue—was the same road that eventually led me to abandon Marxism.

I was placed in solitary confinement, where thinking was my only escape from the terrifying reality. When I had exhausted most topics, it was economics that was my iron reserve. At first I pondered over the theories I knew and compared them. I traced the economic reality from the Depression to the war, and contrasted Soviet and Czechoslovak planning with other systems.

Not long after my imprisonment began, the endless hours of solitary confinement led me to develop a new form of thinking. In normal life one's views are communicated, and through this interaction become reified. During this process, a person usually tries to filter the reality around him through his own conceptual prism, so that his beliefs are reinforced by picking out those facts and phenomena from reality that conform to his perspective. The interaction often ends up by becoming simply an effort to prove the validity of one's views, rather than a search for the truth.

In solitary I was not confronted with these kinds of obstacles, and in this respect I felt far freer than ever before. In the beginning, I compared theories with reality and with each other. I examined which phenomena could be interpreted by different notions, and which of these interpretations seemed more consistent. But I was not content with this level of thinking and began to probe deeper, until I was working with the basic assumptions upon which the theories were based.

At this point I was surprised to find that the basic assumptions underlying the classics of both capitalism and socialism were actually the same, despite their differing conclusions. Furthermore, I found that these assumptions were not "truths," but, rather, guidelines for action. I discovered as well the major role that these fundamental premises play. While we are usually concerned with the contrast between theory and practice, and then with the consistency of these theories, we overlook the importance, and even the existence, of the *basics*. We are not aware that we limit our view of reality by our own particular conceptual prism.

I then realized that what I had previously thought to be a deviation was actually built into the essential principles of Marxism upon which the Soviet model is based. Under the influence of Marxist thought I had come to regard the evils of capitalism (including its fascist form) not as "distortions," not as accidental phenomena, nor as the acts of unworthy people in power, but as inherent in the properties of the capitalist system. This same method of thinking led me to view Stalinism not as a perversion of Marxist philosophy but as an integral part of the system and one of the consequences of the basics of Marxism.

I have mentioned that I was originally fascinated by the philosophy of Marx because his universal dialectical laws, applicable to both society and nature, seemed to lead to a better and a more humane society. Upon probing further into the notion of determinism, however, this time from a humanistic perspective, I found that its application actually destroyed any kind of humanism in society, and that this was equally true for the classics of socialism as for those of capitalism. Determinism as a philosophical category is, in the final analysis, a question of belief. If we accept, as Marx did, the existence of a historical determinism which leads to socialism and to communism, then we must also believe in the existence of an agent which is assigned by history to bring society from capitalism to the higher stages of development. This agent is, in terms of Marxist thought, the proletariat, who as the product and the victim of capitalism must overthrow it to survive.

Once we accept that this historical development is determined, then everything becomes subservient to the class struggle and to the dictatorship of the proletariat. Man's dreams and aspirations do not then become the guide for action, but rather the strategy and tactics required to bring about the victory of the dictatorship of the proletariat. As any dictatorship must have its hierarchy, the leadership of the proletariat—i.e., the party—becomes the source of authoritarian rule.

The same situation flows from the basic assumptions of capitalism, too. Here the motion of the economy is governed by the "invisible hand," or, expressed in more scientific terms, by certain fixed economic laws. It is the "determined" nature of these laws that allows prices to be fixed at levels that provide for profit, that allows the accumulation and concentration of wealth, and that leads to the dictatorship of capital.

While the concept of laws or of determinism may be validly treated as a philosophical issue or as part of the apparatus of the natural sciences, the concept takes on a completely different meaning when applied to the social sciences. If we accept socioeconomic phenomena as determined, then we act accordingly and only reinforce their "deterministic" nature. In other words, if we believe in the concept of laws and interpret occurrences as a function of them, then we behave as if they actually exist, and create situations accordingly. This has a great deal to do with the economic chaos with which we are currently faced.

For instance, when we assert Marx's notion that the law of history is one of class struggle, we are then induced to *create* such a conflict. The believers in this concept, of whom I was one, actually fostered the most militant, ruthless, and inhumane class struggle known in history. We even turned peasants and small shopkeepers into a "class enemy" by persecuting them and their children. The way we categorize influences the way we act.

In the same manner, to bring a more contemporary problem into the picture, capitalist theories accept the existence of a trade-off between unemployment and inflation. If we believe in such a trade-off, then there will be such a trade-off. We will not be concerned with changing the economic and social system; instead, we will perpetuate and reinforce the system by predicting the interdependence of these two phenomena and leaving the conditions responsible for the trade-off unchanged.

The fallacy in deterministic thinking also applies to the notion of ownership. Marx regarded social ownership as the foundation of a humane society, and criticized private ownership as the basis of all evil. On the other hand, the capitalist basic assumption identifies private ownership with freedom. In both cases, the form of ownership becomes the center of consideration, and humanism or anti-humanism only its by-product.

Once such a concept is accepted, nations become divided solely according to the form of ownership. Fascism, Communism, World War II, the cold war, and the balance of power concept are the consequences.

In the realm of the natural sciences, we try to penetrate below appearances and find some principles or working hypotheses which will explain phenomena. There, our thinking is concerned with phenomena which exist independently of man. In the social sciences, however, the social reality is the *creation* of man; it is the result of our ability to think.

Consequently, we can not let concepts of physics—lawfulness, determinism, predictability, quantifiability, etc.—govern our economic actions; it is the way we think and interpret that shapes our economic actions and creations.

The basic assumptions of both capitalism and socialism are the same. Marxism is not a viable alternative to capitalism or the other way around. Consequently, we must be concerned first of all with formulating new fundamental concepts that derive from our true socioeconomic reality.

I have tried, therefore, in this book (which I regard as a synopsis of a more comprehensive study on which I am working) to concentrate on basic concepts and not on individual theories, to suggest the broad outlines of humanomics. I address it to my young colleagues, to students, and to the remarkable number of those who are familiar with economics but are at a loss to understand the roots of our economic and social malaise and would like, at least, to discuss a humane alternative for our society.

I appreciate the assistance of some of my students for their editing of the first draft for the purpose of making it understandable to other students: Jane Hemphill, Stephen Leaderman, Andrew Shapiro, Ben Warren, and Pamela Wilds. Scott Goddard contributed research and editorial assistance on the final draft. My special thanks to Todd Mann, and to James Stark, my research assistants for some years.

PART 1

RETHINKING OUR WORLD

THE SOURCE OF WEALTH

For too long a time now we have been treating the differences between our past and our present as the reasons for our contemporary malaise. It is time we realized that such differences as a higher standard of living, more sophisticated technology, and a higher rate of unemployment and inflation are only *descriptions* of this malaise and not the *causes*. The causes are more deeply embedded within our whole socioeconomic system. We will not be able to eliminate or change the undesirable aspects of our society, in particular our economy, by dealing with symptoms. Rather, we must attempt to understand the reasons for our problems by trying to grasp the *whole* reality of our socioeconomic life.

Understanding the causes, the roots, of economic reality has always been the major starting point for economic philosophies. At the core of all the economic schools of thought lies the fundamental question: "What is the source of wealth?" This question is so essential for economists because it is the means through which they have tried to understand their economy and, indeed, their whole socioeconomic system. In view of our current situation, understanding the source of wealth is just as important today as it was when the first attempt was made over two hundred years ago.

The French physician François Quesnay is regarded as the father of economics; he was the first to view an economy in terms of "source of wealth." As founder of the physiocratic ("rule of nature") school, he saw agricultural labor as this source. According to the physiocrats, "man does not create," he only transforms what nature, the only creator, offers. The physiocrats, in line with their philosophy—and since France was highly agricultural at the time—naturally believed that farm work was the sole creator of wealth. Where the physiocrats truly changed economic thinking was in introducing labor as a fundamental concept. Without labor, they said, there is no wealth and thus no economy.

The classic school of capitalism, particularly its founder, Adam Smith, strongly opposed the view that only farm work is productive. Smith lived in a country that had become the most industrialized and richest in the world. Understanding England's economic reality, he could not accept that agricultural work was the decisive wealth-creating factor. Smith saw the tremendous impact that the growth of industry and labor were having on the economy. He concluded that the division of labor was the basis of industrialization and of the wealth of nations.

Marx followed this philosophy, but from a different perspective. He saw in the division of labor a dehumanizing and alienating means of creating wealth, which, due to the capitalistic character of the socioeconomic system, served to benefit only the owners of the means of production. Emphasizing the point that only labor creates wealth, he reasoned that only those who create the wealth, the working class, should benefit from it and should thereby expropriate the means of production from the owners.

All three schools not only pointed to a source of wealth but prescribed the most efficient use of it as well. Since Quesnay saw society and economy as being part of the natural order, he claimed that the man-made order should respect and not interfere with the natural order.

Quesnay's belief in noninterference was developed by Smith into the philosophy of free enterprise. Smith interpreted economy, as well as society, as the "consequence of a certain propensity in human nature." But even with all the varying "private interests and passions of men," he believed there was an agent, an "invisible hand," which brought all the contradicting actions into a harmony agreeable to the whole society. Respect for the natural order thus received a more scientific name—the invisible hand—and became an economic law. According to the classics, then, optimal performance of the economy could be achieved by letting this invisible hand, or economic law, act without any interference.

Marx agreed with Smith that the source of wealth was to be found in the work of manual labor employed in industry. He also accepted the notion of economic laws being responsible for the performance of the economy. But where Marx deviated from the classics was in the development of his universal dialectical laws. While the laws of the classics were based on private ownership, Marx contended that this form of ownership would inevitably be replaced by social ownership. Social ownership, he reasoned, would be a more just use of the source of wealth, as its creators would be its recipients as well.

However strange it may sound, the question posited by the founders of economics has not been asked again for more than a century. Indeed, the idea of labor being the source of wealth seemed so obvious that it has been accepted as valid outside of time and space. The classical concept of laws has remained the axiom for followers of classical economics, the proponents of contemporary economics. Marx's concept of labor, as well as the role of ownership and the dialectical laws he formulated, are still accepted in Marxian economics.

What has been overlooked since the question of source of wealth was last asked is that the content of this concept has changed. Applied science has replaced manual labor in the transformation of natural forces into productive forces. It is the level of thinking applied to the productive process which has become not only the most dynamic economic factor, but the decisive source of wealth as well. Applied science is the essential factor that accounts for the difference between the old and the new economic reality.

The first and most obvious difference between the old world (before the nineteenth century) and now is that we have at our disposal fantastic resources of energy as a result of our ability to transform natural forces into productive forces. There is no need to prove that this great leap is the result of applying science to production. Science not only discovered new natural forces but, by applying increasingly better technology, it transformed natural forces known to earlier generations to higher levels. This revolutionary leap has been reflected in a most precipitous change of society and economy. It has resulted in a rising standard of living, in the replacement of manual labor by controlled natural forces (or "energy slaves," as Buckminister Fuller called them), and in changing the basic faculties of an economy based on applied science.

Even with a revolutionary mode of production and a fundamentally different socioeconomic reality, we still think in the terms of the past. For instance, Quesnay, as we have seen, assumed that only farms were productive. While he may have overestimated the role of agricultural work, he was right insofar as it was the work of the farmer that fed the whole nation. There was no doubt that the farmer himself produced all the agricultural products.

Is the farmer the sole producer of agricultural products today? If we are not absorbed by appearance and try to see the reality of agricultural production, we will arrive at a completely different answer than we would have even fifty years ago. The farmer in America, for example, produces approximately fifteen times as much as did the farmer in Quesnay's time. Today's farmer produces much more without even having to work as hard. He makes use of chemical fertilizers and many other products of agrochemistry, and has tractors, trucks, and other equipment at his disposal. Yet without these items, he would produce only one-fifteenth of his actual output. We could say, then, that the other fourteen-fifteenths consist of the products of the chemical and machine industries. In other words, modern technology is responsible for the majority of the finished agricultural products.

But who is responsible for the production of modern technology? Is it not the whole system—the mining industry, the machine tool industry, the chemical industry, the educational system, the banking system, the transportation system, etc.? It appears that grain is not the result of the efforts of just the farmers, but of practically all the working strata of society. To say that grain today is produced by labor means something far different than it did in Quesnay's time.

One of the examples Smith used in pointing to labor, and particularly the division of labor, as the source of wealth was his observance of the production of pins. During the time of both Smith and Marx, it was obvious that the worker in the pin factory produced the pin. Today, however, the pin is produced by machines. The extent to which the workers participate in production may vary, but essentially it involves turning the machine on in the morning and turning it off at night. The ensuing question is, then, what kind of and whose labor is actually producing the pin?

The type of labor observed and studied by the classics of capitalism and socialism cannot answer the question, as it does not exist anymore. Yet the theories based on these old concepts still survive. If we are going to understand our contemporary economy, we must clearly understand the source of wealth and the wealth-creating process in a modern economy.

Let us look, for example, at the most primitive agricultural work thousands of years ago. We would see the peasant scraping the earth with some crude tools and planting his kernels of grain. Some months later we would see him reaping a harvest.

What is actually happening when this primitive farmer works is that, as a part of nature, he feels hunger pains if he lacks the means to satisfy his physiological wants. While nature made him hungry, it failed to guarantee that he would always have what he needed for his subsistence. If man was to survive, he had to take from nature what it would not willingly give. Thus, the first step in understanding the essence of work is recognizing this conflict between man and nature.

Taken alone, though, this conflict is not an explanation of labor or the source of wealth. Before man could work, he had to be able to think in terms of cause and effect. Without his ability to think, he never would have been able to discover that he could meet certain needs only by performing certain activities. By finding out that there was a causal nexus between a certain kind of work and a harvest, man's ability to think proved to be a tool making him less dependent upon nature. It is from this angle of man's ability to think that we must approach the process of creating wealth.

LABOR THE TRANSFORMER

The input of our primitive farmer consisted of some seeds plus his work, and the output resulted in a sufficient amount of food for himself and possibly enough to bring up his family. But wealth could not be created unless more was produced—unless a greater output was achieved than that needed for his own and his family's subsistence. In order to achieve this, the farmer had to learn to transform more natural forces into productive forces. He could try to produce more by working more, but this possibility had its natural limitations. Only when, due to his ability to think, he discovered the importance of watering, of preparing the soil, of destroying weeds, and of manure, was he able to transform more natural forces and create a larger harvest.

We can see from just this early and simple stage of labor that increasing production was the result of increasing the intellectual level on which the labor was based. Even with the same input of seed and manual labor, a far greater output was achieved. The source of wealth thus lies in the degree to which we are able to transform and control natural forces, and this, in turn, is a direct result and a function of our ability to think and to create.

All the wealth economics concerns itself with has its basis in (1) the transformation of natural forces into useful forces, natural goods into useful goods, and (2) our ability to mobilize and to transform more natural forces than we originally put in. For instance, if a man designed a water mill, his input would be the work which was quantifiable in terms of time and energy spent. The essence of his work, however, was not the time or energy he put into it but, rather, his creative ability to develop the idea of transforming the flow of water into a useful and controlled force. The water mill made it possible to benefit, to gain from the utility of this transformation process; it created far more energy than had been invested in its development, and this is a fundamental economic activity.

It is most impressive to see that Quesnay, the founder of economic thinking, touched upon the basic question of economic activity in his assumption of the role of nature. He believed that nature created and man only transformed what nature offered, and thus man's creativity consisted of making use of and controlling those natural forces. Although he reduced the transformation process to only agricultural work, he nevertheless was the first to touch upon the essence of work.

It is through understanding the essence of work that we can begin to see the first traces of progress in the productive process. As we have seen, the difference between input and output in the transformation of natural to useful resources is both a function of man's ability to think and of his ability to achieve a higher intellectual level on which the productive process is based. For example, the discovery of the causal relationship between planting some seeds, watering them, and their growing into a harvest created a new intellectual level for the production process that was higher than the previous one. But it also created a higher level of achievement of agricultural work for the future. We are not saying that farmers who apply these discoveries are, as individuals, more intelligent than their predecessors. Rather, they are moving on a plane that is the result of a higher intellectual achievement, working on a level created by the contributions of the generations preceding them.

The key issue is, then, to see that labor is, in essence, a transformation of natural forces and goods, and that this transformation depends on the ability of man to think. Apart from the intellectual contribution of any single worker, the transformation process always takes place on a certain general intellectual level, which is the result of a continuum of creative work of many generations.

THE "GAIN"

If we view labor as the transformation of natural forces into useful ones, and see that this transformation process is the result of its own contemporary intellectual level, then what is involved in the difference between input and output in this process becomes very important. To understand this difference, we have to introduce a new concept into our economic thinking.

The concept of "Gain" expresses the described difference between input and output in the transformation process. "Gain" is materialized in wealth, in a higher standard of living, and in a higher degree of independence from nature, to name a few manifestations. Since the scope of wealth is to be seen in this "gain," we should ask ourselves how and why the scope of "gain" grows.

In the last century the notion of wealth was conceived basically as the accumulation of material possessions. The concept of "gain" transcends this notion of wealth. We can, for example, see radios or television sets as only material possessions, but we can also see a "gain" in them that goes considerably beyond that. The citizen who has a radio or television today has far greater access to information than any government minister or official did just a few generations ago. Similarly, we can view drugs in a pharmacy as mere material objects which will lessen our pain, but more importantly, each product is a "gain" in shortening the duration of an illness and in prolonging our life expectancy.

We have used the concepts of "gain" and of labor (the transformation of natural forces) not just to introduce a "new" concept. Rather, we feel that these concepts are extremely helpful for understanding the reality in which we live and for reorienting our thinking toward the essentials of the mature economy. We can demonstrate how helpful this approach is by using a very realistic example. The world is divided on the concept of the form of ownership. Since the Second World War, the conflict over which form of ownership brings mankind freedom and dignity has resulted in a cold war and the loss of millions of lives. If we look at society from the point of view of "gain," however, we cannot avoid the conclusion that the form of ownership—although its importance should not be neglected—cannot be seen as crucial.

If we see "gain" as a function of man's ability to think, and if we recognize the importance of the intellectual level on which the economy is based, then our prime interest will be oriented toward the development of this level. The form of ownership may be detrimental, instrumental, or neutral, but the standard of living, and we could even say the quality of life, will not be dependent on it, but will be the result of our level of thinking applied to the whole socioeconomic process. The point is, we can *change* our reality toward goals we desire.

THE INTEGRATION OF THE ECONOMY

Besides the transformation process, there is another very essential difference between the old and the new modes of production. When we look at the production of shoes as it existed before the nineteenth century, we find that production was based solely on the work of individual craftsmen. The farmer sold his cowhides to the tanner, the tanner sold his leather to the shoemaker, and the shoemaker sold his finished shoes to the consumer. Shoe production was the result of cooperation between each of these individual units, each of them playing an autonomous role in the transformation process.

Now that shoe production is based on applied science, the process of interaction can no longer be called mere cooperation. The farmer is dependent on a high level of agricultural science in his use of tractors, pesticides, and manure. The tannery and the shoe factory are now complex organisms which utilize the most advanced creations of science and engineering. The production of even a single shoe in a developed economy is contingent on applied science at every stage of production. The mining, metallurgy, machine tool, and chemical industries, for example, are integral elements in the manufacturing of shoes. Complex networks of transportation, banking, and distribution are also necessary. In addition, a system of elementary schools, high schools, universities, and research institutes is important. A type of organization and administration unknown a hundred years ago is an indispensable part of production. Thus, the production of shoes, as an example of modern mass production, is a new phenomenon; the parts that are involved in the production process are interdependent and integrated in a totally new way.

The mature economy represents the complete interdependence of a large number of subsystems and no longer consists of cooperation between discrete and autonomous units. It has merged into a single, incredibly complex and integrated system, which acts as one giant transformer. It is no longer meaningful to talk of voluntary cooperation between autonomous units; production based on applied science is an organic system in which factors of production can neither exist nor be understood in isolation.

A single factory, then, while formally and legally an autonomous unit, is economically speaking not so. The single factory in a modern economy is analogous to a part of the human body. A finger, for example, is a finger in appearance and in function when it is a part of the body. If we remove it, though, it is a finger only in appearance. It has no function when separated from the system of which it is a part.

The analogy to the human system is valid for more than just a single factory. In the not so distant past, the schoolteacher stood outside of the productive process as the farmer, the tanner, and the shoemaker did not need the educational system for their respective products. In contrast, today's gigantic transformer could not have been created and could not continue to perform without the educational system. As the empirical basis of the economy (by this we mean an economy based on experience gained in the working process) was overtaken by applied science, the economy developed into an integrated system, which now includes the active effort of practically all working people. A certain quantity of grain, or a pair of shoes, or any other commodity has become a national product in the sense that it is the result of the effort of the whole nation rather than of one or a group of individuals.

It is important to realize that there is a fundamental difference between the economic system we have described and one which is purely organic. The dissimilarity is that the "cell" of our integrated socioeconomic system is composed of thinking human beings. We must see in society a system of creative people, a system *sui generis* and different from any other system we observe in nature. Therefore, the terms of reference for the scientific discipline dealing with society and economy should be those derived from a science dealing with an order created by thinking human beings.

THE SHARE OF WEALTH

As long as the farmer produced the grain himself, there was no doubt that his work alone produced the value of the product. He could consequently have claimed in payment the full equivalent of what he produced. If, by one way or another, he received less than he produced, he may have felt himself to be exploited.

But the situation today is very different. The farmer is not the only factor involved in the process of grain production. We also have such factors as those people who are responsible for the tractors, fertilizers, transportation, and education. While all of them have contributed to the production of grain, there is no way of determining the share of each in its production. We know that without the educational system, for instance, we would not have the shoe, the car, the grain, and the other commodities. But the teacher's actual share in the gross national product cannot be determined. As a matter of fact, no one would think to ask such a question. No objective means exist by which to attribute a share of the GNP to any individual or branch or stratum, which implies that there is no objective way to state the rewards for work.

It is important to understand that today we cannot know how much any worker has contributed to the value of a product. The labor theory of value first formulated by David Ricardo assumed that the value of a commodity was equal to the amount of labor needed to produce it. As long as manual labor was the standard means of production, such an idea was at least logical. But applied science and the multitude of factors determining production have rendered this theory inapplicable. Marx accepted Ricardo's theory and claimed that the worker should receive the full value of what he produced. In Marx's time, perhaps, the full value of the product could be objectively traced to the worker. In a mature economy this is impossible. There is no objective way to fix the share of any kind of labor on a commodity.

Economists attempt to deal with objective data; wages and salaries are treated objectively by those receiving payments, by those paying the rewards, and by statisticians. Yet, in reality, rewards cannot be viewed in this way. We must be aware that rewards for work, and even rewards for no work, are the results of conventions sometimes agreed upon and very often imposed. Our daily lives show us that final agreements on rewards are frequently the result of conflicts and strikes. From this we can see that economists who view wages and rewards objectively are ignoring what is essentially a subjective economic reality. The only quantifiable element we can know is what collective manual and mental labor has produced in terms of the GNP.

Similarly, as all prices consist of rewards (sales, salaries, profits, taxes), they also do not express an objective relationship with the GNP. If the GNP is 1,000 billion units, for example, and a car costs 10,000 units, mathematically it means that the car is 1/100-million of the GNP. As with the price of labor, the actual share of the car in the GNP, however, cannot be reflected in its price. Consequently, we must also treat prices as not being fixed in an objective manner.

Yet prices *are* treated as objectively and in the same manner as the natural sciences deal with physical phenomena. Prices are objectified and viewed by economists in terms of laws, graphs, and equations, when in actuality they are, by their very nature, subjective entities. The prices of labor and goods cannot be regarded as quantifiable phenomena in the same way that a physicist views the law of gravitation. Prices and rewards are created and determined by man, whereas natural phenomena exist independently of him.

Once we realize that rewards and prices are not made by laws and that they are not the result of curves and sophisticated equations, then we can begin to determine them and their criteria. Naturally, the formulation of the criteria for the value of rewards is a subjective task. It will demand taking into consideration such humane elements as just and dignified rewards, rewards which make the work effort attractive, and rewards which provide incentive.

With regard to prices, we should no longer assume that changing prices, which are usually manifested in inflation, are the results of laws or objective factors. Inflation is justified by existing theories as an inevitable consequence of boom and of full employment. One such theory is exemplified by the Phillips Curve. This theory states that high employment creates high inflation and stable prices create unemployment. The Phillips Curve is a "proof" that changing prices and/or unemployment are objective and inevitable phenomena. This is not the case, however. Whether we create a system of stable prices or whether we face a state of permanent inflation is up to us.

WHO OWNS THE MEANS OF PRODUCTION?

When Smith and Marx were alive, it was easy to determine who owned a factory or a business. Even today, it seems as self-evident as it was over two hundred years ago. The only difference between owning a water mill then and a hydroturbine engine today, it is conventionally agreed, is that the owner of the latter is richer than that of the former. From the legal point of view as well, no great change has occurred. The owner of the means of production can still decide to sell his business, decide what he will and will not produce, and decide how to make use of his ownership. He is regarded as the sole and autonomous owner.

Despite the minor differences on the surface, however, there has been a far-reaching change in the essence of ownership. To understand this change, let us again take a closer look at the factory as it was many years ago and as it exists in today's economy. If somebody a hundred years ago produced coaches, his factory was an autonomous unit and could be seen in every respect to belong solely to him. But this is not the case with a modern automobile plant. As we concluded earlier, this plant is a part of an integrated system and should be seen as one of the many subsystems. As in the analogy to the finger, it is a part of a system outside of which it cannot exist. Although its properties and functions are most specific, we should see the car plant as a part that is "nourished" by the whole system of which it is a component.

The existence of the modern car factory is contingent upon a system of roads and highways, the oil industry, and the machine tool industry. The extent to which the car factory is developed depends on and parallels the level of the above-mentioned industries as well as that of education and research. We must also remember that the achievements of previous generations are also incorporated in the production of the car. All of these factors which have contributed to today's car production are not always noticed, because the emergence of the modern automobile plant is the result of a long evolutionary process.

Take the example of a planned economy which has just begun industrialization and whose planners have decided to build a car factory. In order to produce cars the economy would also have to invest in education and research facilities, in road building, and in the many industries connected with car production. While it is possible to assess the cost of building the factory, it is impossible to determine the cost of the whole intellectual, economic, and social infrastructure. These factors are the less conspicuous elements which contribute to the growth of the car industry.

The concept of economy as an organic system, then, makes it clear that it is not one person alone who owns or is responsible for the means of production. Ownership of the means of production today is actually a type of "joint tenancy" ownership, because society contributes just as much as, if not more than, the actual owner. (This does not necessarily apply to many small businesses, but it does apply to those larger ones collectively responsible for approximately 90% of the GNP.) While the owner of a factory pays his workers, designers, and administrators, the education of the workers and the study of new techniques in designs and management science are investments of the whole nation.

This phenomenon needs to be recognized. The owner of a factory or business is making full use of the economic, social, and cultural infrastructure which society has developed and paid for. This is why the ownership of the means of production has become a kind of joint ownership. Yet the general economic perspective, existing theories, and legislatures view the concept of ownership only as the sole ownership of a discrete unit. It is not taken into consideration that no business exists or functions as an autonomous unit or that these businesses are being nurtured by "capital" which belongs to the nation as a whole.

Marx assumed that if the workers expropriated the means of production from the owners, then the source of all social evils would disappear. But as we have seen, only the final phase of shoe production takes place in the shoe factory. Marx did not see that shoe production is an integrated effort of most of the branches of society. He reasoned only that the working class should benefit from the production and not the owners. The application of Marxism leads to government ownership of the means of production. But once the government becomes the owner of the means of production, it ceases to be the organ of the nation. Instead it becomes the sole employer of the nation, which becomes in every respect dependent on the government.

Whereas we used to think in terms of whether viable alternatives are provided by private or socialist ownership, we must think in completely different terms now that we see that "joint tenancy" ownership is typical for the modern economy. The crucial issue is how this new form of ownership will be applied to contemporary means of production. If we accept the form of ownership that is conceived of in mixed economies, if we think in terms of workers being the owners or of government ownership, we are moving toward a dead end because we are dealing with concepts of ownership that do not exist in reality.

If we think in terms of this new concept of ownership, however, then we can regard the owner of the means of production, whoever it might be, as a kind of trustee who uses the nation's "capital." The government, as the organ of the nation, can then act as the protector of the "capital" of the nation. It should be an obligation of the government to insure that the individual rights of ownership also include fulfilling the duties of ownership to the nation, in other words, to the "joint tenancy" owners of the means of production.

As we have seen, the underlying concepts of ownership of the means of production have become outdated. It should therefore not be surprising that attempted solutions to our socioeconomic problems based either on changing the form of ownership or on maintaining the status quo have failed to bring any of the desired results. The concept of "joint tenancy" ownership is one of the properties of an economy based on applied science. In order to derive further conclusions from this new concept, we will have to inquire further into the nature of this type of economy.

THE LUCROACTIVITY OF SCIENCE

As a consequence of applied science, we have created a new kind of "gain" which is a counterpart to the new phenomenon of "social" ("joint tenancy") ownership. Let us therefore turn our attention to the interaction of "gain" and "social" ownership.

The Puzzle of Rip Van Winkle

When shoes were produced solely by manual labor, the production of one pair of shoes (including the labor of the farmer, tanner, and dyer, etc.) required, say, sixty hours of manual labor. In buying a pair of shoes, then, a consumer was paying the equivalent of sixty hours worth of wages, plus extra for taxes and profits. In contrast, a consumer in the United States in 1971 could purchase a pair of shoes for the equivalent of six hours (average) worth of wages, plus the addition of taxes and profits.

The difference between the cost of a pair of shoes today and the same pair a hundred years ago is more than just a change in price; the difference represents a qualitative change in the way "gain" is materialized. To further clarify this basic change in the economy, here is an idealized situation.

Let us suppose that Rip Van Winkle had slept for a hundred years instead of twenty. Further, let us suppose that he had been on his way to buy a pair of shoes when he fell asleep, so that, upon waking up, his first thought is to buy some shoes. Coming to a shoe store, he offers to work sixty hours in exchange for the shoes (that is, the amount of work he had done the last time he had bought a pair of shoes a hundred years ago). To his surprise, he learns that he needs to work only six hours to earn them. Naturally, he wonders who will do the fifty-four hours of additional work which previously needed to be done in order to purchase a pair of shoes.

It may be absolutely inconceivable to him that he has received the benefit of the equivalent of fifty-four hours free of charge. Before he went to sleep, he thought that only when someone worked (or let someone work for him) could he gain. He was convinced that any benefit, like profit, could accrue only to the business. Yet, he sees that he, as a consumer, has gained the equivalent of fifty-four hours, while the producer has gained only his profit from the price, or a fraction of the equivalent of six working hours. Rip Van Winkle will, of course, desire to know how this is possible, and it will be explained to him that during these hundred years new technology has been developed, more capital has been invested, and the productivity of labor has grown. Still, it will be difficult to explain why the producer has gone through all this effort to create a situation where the consumer has such a benefit.

During this explanation he will find that the average consumer is not interested in the fact that a hundred years ago there was a different ratio between wages and the price of shoes. More likely, the purchaser thinks (if he thinks in these terms at all) that shoes now cost six hours' wages. In fact, the average consumer buys shoes feeling that he has paid a price equal to their value without realizing that he has benefitted anything at all. Rip Van Winkle, dissatisfied with the answers he has received, may turn to economics. In doing so, he will probably be pleasantly surprised to find that basically the same economics exist today as those he read a hundred years earlier. Although he may find some new equations and graphs, he will not find an answer to his question. Let us offer him one.

The production of shoes, whatever the kind of labor and at whatever stage in the history of man, has always been a transformation of natural forces into productive forces and of natural goods into useful goods. As long as this transformation process was based on thinking derived only from the experience of the working process, the "gain" was relatively small. For instance, if the shoemaker employed a few workers, he may have kept a part of the "gain" produced by the workers. In this case, the "gain" materialized in the realm of the producers.

Once we apply science to the productive process, we are transforming natural forces into "energy slaves" and letting them do the work for us. Involved in the production of a pair of shoes, then, is six hours of work by human beings and fifty-four hours of work by energy slaves. We do not pay for the energy slaves, because the six hours of work already includes their transformation from natural forces. The energy slaves work on the farm in the form of tractors. As chemical fertilizers, they transform biochemical forces with the help of chemical fertilizers. They work for us in the mining industry, the machine tool industry, and the factory where machinery for the shoe industry is produced. We employ energy slaves in the chemical industry to produce chemicals for the tannery and shoe production. Energy slaves at work in the transportation system make the distribution of the shoes possible. The result of this type of transformation process is the mass production of shoes. Compared with shoes some hundred years ago, the price today, expressed in terms of working hours, is approximately one-tenth of what it was.

We can see in this simplified example that the "gain" of the transformation process is not being materialized only in the sphere of the producer. The producer of the shoes may, owing to the fact that he produces millions of pairs of shoes, have a high profit. If his profit, for example, is the equivalent of one working hour for each million pairs of shoes produced, then his total profit is equivalent to one million working hours. Even though the producer continues, as he always has, to make a profit, it is an entirely new phenomenon that the "gain" which radiates into the sphere of the consumer is far greater than that of the producer. Without applied science, everyone would still have to pay the equivalent of sixty working hours for a pair of shoes, and it is doubtful that enough shoes would be produced to enable everyone to buy one pair even every three years. The radiation of "gain" into the area of consumption, although not at all obvious, is typical for any economy based on applied science.

Try to picture the American economy without applying science to production; more than half of its population would be condemned to death and the rest would live at best at the subsistence level. Without applied science, we would not have such benefits as electricity, railways, cars, planes, radios, televisions, health services, plentiful grain, and widespread education, to name just a few. The increase in the standard of living is actually materialized "gain." We must especially emphasize the point that the "gain," which accrues through transformation based on applied science, has the inherent quality of radiating into the whole society and should, therefore, be seen as social.

This phenomenon—that "gain" has the fundamental property of radiating into all pores of the sphere of consumption and of being inherently social—we call *the lucroactivity of science*. (In Latin, *lucrum* means "gain." The concept of activity is borrowed from radioactivity, the spontaneous emission of radiation of unstable atomic nuclei as a consequence of a nuclear reaction.)

We meet the phenomenon of lucroactivity wherever we look in our daily lives. A simple comparison between our standard of living and that of the early nineteenth century would demonstrate it. Or we could compare a country which is developed because it has applied science to production to an underdeveloped country which hasn't. The real difference lies in two factors. The first is the extent and role of the level of thinking on which the production process is based. The second is the effect of applied science in creating "social gain." We must recognize that this "social gain" must be protected, as it is the result of the nation's working effort and belongs, by its very nature, to the nation.

Once we have applied science to production, we realize that along with technology, we also need organization, management, and banking systems in order to produce. Just as important as technology is the level of thinking on which businesses base their own microeconomic policies. The effect of lucroactivity depends on the level of the macroeconomy as well. If we are unable to supply the consumer with enough income to buy what we could potentially produce, then we are not making use of the potential of the lucroactivity, and we are depriving the country of the "gain" it is entitled to have.

Depriving the nation of "gain" can occur under any form of ownership. The decisive problem is the level of thinking on which the productive and managerial processes are based and the social and economic relations that are then formed from this base. The role of the government should be a congruous one with regard to the economy. The experience in all developed countries proves that interference of the government into the economic performance of businesses leads to an overbureaucratization and an undermining of their ability to function efficiently. This causes them great economic harm. On the other hand, noninterference of the government into the economy causes even greater damage. The fact that individual businesses are part of an integrated system makes it necessary to take measures with regard to the performance of the system. This can be done only by a macroorgan like the government.

In protecting that part of the economy which belongs to the nation, i.e., the "gain," the government is protecting its potential recipients, the consumers. This task is complex: how to optimize this "gain"; how to support any attempt to make the economic performance of business more effective; how to make full use of the economic potential; and how to make what can potentially be produced available to all consumers. The government will have to have a guide for the advice and tools necessary to fulfill this task. This means the government will need economists who will accept the study of the optimization of the performance of the whole economy as their frame of reference.

In later chapters I will present some ways of approaching this task.

THE SYSTEM AND ITS ORIENTATION

We have seen that it is important to view the economy as a system of human beings that has a level of thinking as its fundamental variable. We concluded, as well, that the economy has developed into a kind of organic, integrated system. In fact, the concept of a system is at the foundation of economic thinking and economics.

As mentioned earlier, Quesnay saw society and its economy as a part of a natural order. In his opinion, this natural order should be respected by man and should not be interfered with by the man-made order (*l'ordre positif*). Hence, the concept of "laissez faire, laissez passer," the philosophy of liberalism, developed. The founder of the classical school, Adam Smith, saw the "invisible hand" as turning all the varying actions of the economic agents into a harmonious system. Since the individual actions of these agents should therefore be seen and interpreted within the framework of the "invisible hand" system, Smith concluded, this system should not be interfered with through extraneous actions.

The followers of Smith further developed this same philosophy of "laissez faire." They interpreted the "invisible hand" as economic laws, and they saw the economy as a system governed by laws. Marx pursued this interpretation of laws. He believed that these laws were part of a larger scope of universal laws which were dialectical by their nature and which determined the motion of nature and society. The form of private ownership divided the society into classes. According to Marx, the classes of owners and workers, as dialectical antitheses, would bring about a synthesis of a classless, socialist society due to the inevitability of a natural historic process.

At the time of Smith and Marx, the Newtonian approach to natural phenomena had developed into a world view applied to any field which was seen as having the potential for scientific study. The scientific ideal, as well as the scientific methodology, was characterized by the reduction of any phenomenon to its smallest component. The relationship of the isolated components would be studied for their causal effects and would then be used as an explanation for the behavior of the phenomenon. This method has been referred to as atomism and mechanism. It is this atomistic and mechanical approach to economy that prevents us from seeing economy as an integrated system and makes us believe we are part of a determined world.

While, in a chemical system, we can mechanistically reduce water to its elements of hydrogen and oxygen, this method is unthinkable in the life sciences. A human body should not be seen as a mere sum of its parts. Rather, it should be seen from the perspective that every organ functions only as a part of the body. We face a similar phenomenon in the economy. Government policies, monetary and fiscal policies, the banking system, education, etc. are all integral to the functioning of the world economic system. We must therefore apply a holistic method in our approach to the economy. We should see the functioning of the system as a whole and study its subsystems (its single organs) with their specific functions, but always with regard to the performance of the system as a whole.

Because our system is made up of thinking human beings, and because applied science is responsible for the system's integrated structure, the behavior of the system, its function, and its orientation depends on the level of thinking on which it is based. How much a worker earns is the result of the level of thinking on which production and the economy as a whole are based. The form of ownership is not a decisive factor. The extent of pollution in our environment is not dependent on the form of ownership but on the principles and the organization of the economy. Whether technology turns against man or serves man, and whether we have unemployment and inflation or full employment and stable prices, are not contingent upon the form of ownership nor on the subjective quality of the economic factors. This is a startling fact to recognize, because implicit in this awareness is the understanding that man can create his economic system and can choose his alternatives.

Economy and society are a creation of man, the result of his creative genius. The ability to think, to feel, and to will is unique to each human being. Our economic and social activities are the result of these unique faculties. Man is to be the measure of all values and considerations. Knowing this, we must not be satisfied any longer with economic laws which supposedly govern us. We must realize that we have the ability to design our world, to make it serve us. Humanomics is based on that realization.

How do we design our world and move toward our goals? Any dynamic and moving phenomenon has a vector of its own movement. The social system has its own vector as well, which we call its orientation. This concept of orientation expresses a direction toward a goal. It does not imply a final, built-in goal. Either we will consciously direct our society toward a desired end, or we leave the orientation of our society to be the result of uncontrollable forces. As we are the creators of our socioeconomic system, we have the ability to choose its orientation and to design our socioeconomic life as we want it to be. Conventional economics does not deal with a designed but with a determined world.

Perhaps it is justifiable to ask whether the subject matter conventional economics deals with exists at all. If we accept the notion that the economy is a man-made system and not governed or controlled by laws, then an economic system governed by laws (the approach used by conventional economics) does not exist. But the answer is not as simple as this. If we believe that our economy is part of a determined world and that all actions are determined to have happened, then we are actually participating in the creation of a determined world. For example, if we accept the trade-off between unemployment and inflation as a determined phenomenon, then this trade-off will always occur and can always be predicted. On the other hand, if we do not think in terms of a determined world, we will assume that this trade-off is a result of our shortcomings, and we will try to create a situation with full employment and no inflation.

Thus, the question of whether our society and economy are our creations or part of the determined universe is not a mere search for truth. It is far more a philosophy which will guide our action. If we accept the philosophy of determinism, then our society will be governed by determined phenomena. On the other hand, if we view society as our creation, then we will be able to control and create the future instead of only predicting it.

In facing a dehumanizing orientation of our economy with its ensuing malaise, we must ask, "Who is responsible?" The apologists claim that economics cannot be blamed, just as medicine cannot be blamed for not having yet discovered a cure for cancer. The proper answer is that economics is responsible for our "cancer." The philosophy on which conventional economics is based eliminates the human dimension and is responsible for the antihuman orientation of the economy. We are faced with *the* crucial question of economics. Will economics continue to develop along the lines of a philosophy based on a determined world governed by objective laws, or will we develop a humanomics based on the principle that economy is a creation of man and, consequently, its orientation can be controlled by man?

PART 2

THE FALLACIES
OF ECONOMICS

THE FALLACY OF
THE DEFINITION
OF ECONOMICS

Economists today agree on a general definition of economics something like the following:

> Economics is the study of how man and society end up choosing, with or without the use of money, to employ scarce productive resources which could have alternative uses, to produce various commodities and distribute them for consumption, now or in the future, among various people and groups in society.[1]

Implicit in this definition is a statement about how men and society *choose* among *scarce* resources (such as beef, wheat, overcoats, bombers), and, after having produced them, how they distribute them for consumption.

This statement is the essence of conventional economics. It reveals the method of analysis and the formulation of the

[1] This quotation can be found on page 4 of Professor Paul Samuelson's *Economics* (McGraw-Hill Book Company, 8th Edition, 1970). This book is the most widely read textbook on economics.

basic assumptions of economics. It also demonstrates *how far removed* economics is from reality. Everybody knows that capital, land, and goods are allocated by households, firms, and "society." However, defining economic reality in this way implies that the economy is seen only as an entity in which men and society end up choosing to employ scarce resources.

To see in any economy primarily the process of allocation is to abstract the main and typical feature of economic performance and to reduce a multidimensional economy to a single dimension. We can demonstrate how oversimplified this perception is in both the most primitive and the most mature economy.

The primitive peasant had to allocate part of his harvest for consumption and the remainder for seeds. This type of allocation, however, describes only one dimension of a larger process. The peasant still had to till the soil, water it, make some tools, as well as apply the experience of many generations. The allocation of his harvest cannot be isolated; it is only a part of the working process of production.

A farmer in a mature economy may also "allocate," but this concept of allocation is not the same, as it is part of a fundamentally different economy. Granted, he will have to allocate part of his capital for tractors, other machinery, and fertilizers, but this allocation is only possible at a stage of development in which we are producing these goods. This is an important difference, because allocation has become subject to primarily technological factors which involve production in other areas of the economy.

Let us look at the production of tractors for example. The process of choosing scarce resources does not produce the tractor. Rather, the allocation is derived from the design of the tractor. From the basis of the design, management decides what has to be ordered. Thus, we can see that allocation is first of all a technological question. But the allocation process does not end here. According to the design of the tractor, machinery has to be ordered. To meet this allocation, the machine tool industry has to, in turn, order the raw material and energy to manufacture the tractors. At all the stages of this process, we find complicated organizations, research facilities, and designers. All of these factors *had* to be developed in order for the tractor to be produced. We can see, therefore, that scarce resources are not a primary concern in allocation. Allocation, in being derived from design, has become primarily a technological concern directly related to a complicated process of production.

The conventional definition of economics has reduced this complex process to a simple act of allocation, which in its isolated form is absolutely meaningless. Who would dare define painting or poetry as the allocation of colors and words? Reducing the economy to this level means that the performance of the economy as a whole is neglected.

WHO ALLOCATES?

In a planned economy such as the Soviet Union's the process of allocation is clear. The planning body knows which scarce resources are available or are supposed to be available. The body, according to general instructions from the Politburo, allocates the resources, be they labor, raw material, capital goods, or credit to ministries such as the ministries of mining, heavy industry, the machine tool industry, etc. These ministries break down the global allocation to factories or groups of factories. (Ironically, Soviet economists define economics not as the study of the allocation of scarce resources, but as the study of economic laws.)

Although the Soviet Union's planned economy demonstrates that there is a specific body which actually allocates, it is an oversimplification to identify even the planned economy simply as the allocation of scarce resources. There is more to it, as we shall see later.

WHO ALLOCATES IN A MIXED ECONOMY?

When we say that society allocates, we are referring to the government. If the government decides to allocate part of the budget in the space program, can we then say that economics is a study of how the government allocates and of the impact of its decisions? Can economists just study why the government has chosen to employ capital for the production of missiles as an "alternative use"? These topics are not at all concerned with economic performance; they are, rather, descriptions of economic decision-making and of the impact of these decisions.

The stock market should provide a relevant source of study for the allocation of capital. Yet, Samuelson quotes Bernard Baruch's caution when looking at the stock market:

> If you are ready to give up everything else to study the whole history and background of the market and all the principal companies whose stocks are on the board as carefully as a medical student studies anatomy—if you can do all that, and in addition, you have the cool nerves of a gambler, the sixth sense of a clairvoyant, and the courage of a lion, you have a ghost of a chance.[2]

We see that economic performance is not taken into consideration in studying the allocation of capital in the stock market. Why should we assume that it is taken into consideration in other capital markets?

[2] Ibid., p. 256.

As far as the allocation of labor is concerned, labor is acknowledged to be a scarce resource, yet it is not treated as such. Unemployment, i.e., the *non*allocation of labor as a scarce resource, is one of the main problems of our economy. Actually, then, the nonallocation of scarce resources can be *just as important* as the allocation of them. The definition of economics does not take this into account.

Is the consumer, in buying a car, the one who allocates or is it the producer of the car? The producer of the car orders steel, glass, and tires. Factories allocate material in order to produce what for them is the final product, but what is for the car producer only the raw material or a spare part.

We could say that the impulse for allocation is first given by the expectation of how the consumer will behave; at a later stage, the behavior of the consumer may influence a change in the allocation process. For instance, if consumers do not allocate enough money for cars, then production would decrease, and this would affect allocation. But the fact that the consumer buys a car means that he allocates part of his own assets.

It seems, then, that it is basically the consumer who allocates. He allocates his "scarce resource," i.e., money, and, accordingly, the producer assigns resources. The consumer may allocate his money and buy a car or TV set, but in order to be able to make this allocation, there is more involved than just having the purchasing power. A fantastic scientific development and its application had to precede the production of the car and TV set. The economic, cultural, scientific, and social infrastructure had to be built up for generations to make it possible first to produce a TV set, then to buy it with the equivalent of a few weeks' wages.

No doubt everybody allocates—the consumer his money and the investor his capital. The producer of steel allocates ore, coal, energy, and labor. But we know that with the same allocation of scarce resources, the economic results can differ according to the design, the level on which the enterprises operate, macroeconomic decisions, and a multitude of other factors. Thus, the "allocation of scarce resources" is only one element of many factors economics needs to study.

Behind this definition of economics is a tendency to make economics into a "science" using "scientific methods" similar to Newton's treatment of physical phenomena. In order to apply this method, a definition was "invented" which made economy fit into this mechanistic world view. (The famous British economist Joan Robinson coined the phrase "to ape natural sciences.") We should see and understand that this definition is a logical and necessary consequence of this world view, but is not really applicable to today's economic reality.

The view that economy is part of the determined world on the same order as physics tends to narrow down our angle of observation to that which is quantifiable. The allocation of resources is quantifiable; the "heart of a lion and the sixth sense of a clairvoyant" are not. The number of TV sets and all its labor input and material are quantifiable. But what really matters—applied science, organization, the intellectual and technical infrastructure, and other essential factors that are responsible for the production of a television— are not at all quantifiable.

According to Pythagoras—and it applies as well to Newton and to contemporary economics—what is not quantifiable doesn't exist. Therefore, it seemed important to formulate a definition of the economy that would use a set of terms based on quantification and leave out all other factors, however essential. This generally accepted definition of economics demonstrates to what degree economics is divorced from reality. We assume that economics is the study of the economy. If the definition states that economics is the study of allocation, there are two explanations. Either the authors do realize that economy is far more than allocation, and they are prepared to disregard everything which is outside of and beyond allocation, or they really feel that economy is nothing more than the choosing of scarce resources. In both cases, we see the degree of divorce from reality.

The crisis of economics, which is responsible for the socioeconomic crisis of our day, is not due to any shortcoming of economists, nor to the lack of their knowledge or sophistication. It is due to these basic tenets of economics, including its frames of reference. The great battle to overcome this crisis of economics will have to take place on the battlefield of basic assumptions. In physics, we cannot but observe nature, study natural processes, and try to use this knowledge either for or against man. Nature exists independently of us, existed before man, and will exist after everything we have created may disappear. But society and economy do not exist without man. They are our own creations, and we have achieved a stage of development where the momentum of the social and economic system needs to be controlled; otherwise, the system might ruin its creators.

We should decide whether we will be satisfied just to "observe" the existing orientation, or whether we want to control it. The economy could be oriented toward profit, toward power, toward the interests of the producers, or toward human interests. It could be geared toward maximum growth of the GNP or toward optimum quality of life. There is no reason why we should be exposed to a situation which destroys our natural environment, a situation which is detrimental to the quality of our lives.

If we see the economy as a human system created by us, we will be able to approach it as its creator and will be able to look for scientific tools which will advise us of the rational alternative directions open to us and the measures to take in order to pursue the many alternative goals.

To be able to control the development of the economy,

we need a science *sui generis*, as different in method from the physical sciences as it is in subject matter. The task would still be to study the past and present economic processes, not as an end in themselves, but rather as a point of departure. Control in the development and orientation of our society would thus become the center of our considerations and the frame of reference.

In one sense, the problem of economics is similar to that of natural science. The development of natural science as an autonomous discipline was a long process, beginning perhaps with Roger Bacon. Before natural science formulated its frame of reference and developed into a science of its own, it had to free itself from the philosophy that was regarded as the "science of all sciences" which preceded it. Economics will likewise have to free itself from the impact of natural science, which is regarded as the "science of all sciences."

The famous British physicist William Kelvin remarked that "ether, an all-pervading, massless medium, indefinitely elastic, seen as a medium of electromagnetic waves, is the only substance scientists are confident of in dynamics. One thing we are sure of and that is the reality and substantiality of the luminiferous ether." Albert Einstein, in his *Physics*, remarked that physicists at the beginning of our century were prepared to give up any concept but ether. A whole world view, that of Newtonian physics, was based on the "fallacy" of ether. The concept of ether had to be abandoned in order to transcend the world view of the past century and to open an avenue to a new age.

The definition of economics reflects the existence of "ether" not yet dethroned. It is a most solid tie to the eighteenth century which economics, despite its sophistication, basically has not transcended today. It must be dethroned in order to create an economics that is capable of serving as a scientific guide toward humane goals.

THE FALLACY OF AN ECONOMICS OUT OF TIME AND SPACE

The logical consequence of seeing an economy in terms of the definition mentioned in the preceding chapter is to view an economy as an absolute, a phenomenon outside of time and space. Resources have to be allocated in all kinds of economies, but by being taught to reduce an economy to one, and by far not the most basic dimension, students learn to look at an economy as something absolute. They are taught to believe that it exists independently of history, as a star does. They learn that at the foundation of every society, there will always be a few universal economic conditions, as crucial today as they were "in the days of Homer and Caesar, and they will continue to be relevant in the brave new world of the future."[1]

The fact that every society is composed of human beings and that perhaps the essence of human nature has not changed over the centuries may create some basic conditions. But regarding these conditions as being as crucial as

[1] Samuelson, *Economics*, p. 15.

they were in the days of Homer and Caesar does not enable us to study our current reality. In order to understand our contemporary economy and society, it is important and necessary to concentrate on the fundamental differences between the past and the present.

Students are taught that "any society, whether it consists of a totally collectivized communist state, a tribe of South Sea Islanders, a capitalistic industrial nation, a Swiss Family Robinson, or perhaps even a colony of bees,"[2] must deal with three basic problems of economic organization. "What" commodities shall be produced, "how" they are to be produced, and "for whom" are questions each society must somehow confront.

There seems to be nothing wrong with this trio. After all, any purposeful action means a "what," a "how," and a "for whom." Even a child playing in the sand and building a castle decides *what* he is going to build, *how*, and *for whom*, whether for himself or for his little sister. That every society must confront these three questions is a truism.

Expressing this truism as a definitional statement for "any society" implies that the economy of a primitive tribe is, in essence, the same as that in America. However, the "what," "how," and "for whom" in a tribal society refer to a completely different socioeconomic reality than the one in our contemporary developed society. It is true that the three questions, as well as the answers to them, are built-in parts of each system. But a modern and a tribal society are such different phenomena that any comparison of them is absolutely irrelevant to any real understanding of each of their economic formations. These questions and the definition of conventional economics, however, force us to make such comparisons.

Students are exposed to the same problem of confusing

2 Ibid., p. 15.

formula with reality when they learn that the choices available to a society are determined by existing technological knowledge combined with limited land, labor, and capital. Every society uses technological knowledge in land, labor, and capital. Nothing can be learned or understood about a tribal society or America from this description because it ignores a tremendous qualitative difference between the two societies. For example, on one spot of land a tribe may be able to produce only a certain vegetable. But in America, many different kinds of vegetation can be produced by applying agrochemical knowledge. The qualitative difference which enables us to understand the economy of these two societies is derived from the intellectual level on which each society is based. Stating that available choices are determined by technological knowledge and limited amounts of scarce resources is a fallacious attempt at turning a creative process unique to each society into a universal condition.

When Samuelson says that population, or the human element, is the basis of any economy, he is treating human beings only as an aggregate in order to establish past and future population trends. Man is quantified like any other economic category. With this approach, students never learn that it is precisely this "human element" which creates economy and is responsible for our socioeconomic life.

The basic fallacy of teaching economics as existing out of time and space is that we must be satisfied with just observing it, rather than seeing man's role in creating it. The first task of economics is, according to Samuelson, "to explain and to correlate the behavior of production, unemployment, prices, and similar phenomena," even though, "because of the complexity of human and social behavior, we cannot attain the precision of the physical sciences."[3] This is the problem with the current approach to economics: we are trying

[3] Ibid., p. 6.

to be precise in our observation of a system which, due to its human nature, cannot be analyzed in this way.

Although Samuelson warns that we should not "slavishly imitate physics," we still treat economics as a natural science rather than as a social one. In order to demonstrate how deep-rooted this philosophy is in our generation of economists, we shall deal further with some aspects of the natural sciences, particularly Newtonian physics. This is all the more important to discuss, as many economists are not aware and even vehemently deny that they think in terms of the "physics of economy." However, as they actually do see and conceive of economy through the prism of "physics," they can only be assuming that what they are observing is the reality. "Dethroning" this method of thinking is the greatest need if we are to understand our economic reality.

THE FALLACIES OF
ECONOMIC LAWS

Many economists contend that if there is a resemblance between certain concepts of economics and physics, it is accidental and of no principal importance. There is more than just a resemblance, however. Let us briefly turn our attention to some of the basic principles of the natural sciences, for examining the development of these principles around the turn of the century is instructive in understanding the crisis of economics.

The natural sciences developed from the basic assumption of the existence of universal natural laws and a universal harmony. This meant that a balanced, stable, and, as a whole, unchanging system existed. This state—one of equilibrium governed by natural laws—became the basic frame of reference for the natural sciences.

Many thinkers view the great tragedians of ancient Greece—Aeschylus, Sophocles, Euripides—with their vision of fate as the predecessors of the vision of scientists. "Fate in Greek tragedy" became, according to Alfred Whitehead, "the order of nature in modern thought."

In the same way that man's actions were to be understood in the context of his fate and his fate understood in the context of his actions, "fate" also became a belief of scientists. Any occurrence was seen as determined and correlated with its antecedents. With this belief in causality and predictability, general principles of laws could be formulated. Throughout the nineteenth century, this philosophy dominated physics. Physics, and all fruitful knowledge, was based upon the conviction that an occurrence in the past leads to particular occurrences in the future.

This same philosophy is at the basis of the scientific world of Newton. He saw the universe as having perfect symmetry and an absolute precision. As everything had its natural and knowable efficient cause, the knowledge of its present and, therefore, of its future was in man's reach. Further, everything was determined and objective, no human act or intervention influenced its behavior. It was a world devoid of all purpose.

While the Copernican revolution dislodged man from the center of the universe, Galileo and Newton removed him totally. Only primary qualities (numbers, figures, magnitude, position, motion) were real; secondary qualities perceived by man (tastes, colors, happiness, odors) were unreal. The latter were names and would disappear if man disappeared. Galileo and Newton explained nature, and man as part of nature, in terms of body and motion.

René Descartes pursued this line of thinking by saying that nature was a machine without purpose or spiritual significance. Thomas Hobbes saw reasoning and imagination as only motions in certain parts of the organic body. For him, only matter existed and everything could be predicted with exact laws. Baruch Spinoza saw the universe as a relentless chain of effects without final cause. He considered human actions and desires in the same manner as if they were lines, planes, and solids. For Pierre Laplace, all phenomena were subsumed in a giant universal mechanism, and what did not fit was only superstition.

J. Robert Oppenheimer describes this world of thought in his *Science and Common Understanding*[1]:

> There was the belief that in the end all nature would be reduced to physics, to the giant machine. Despite all richness of what men have learned about the world of nature, of matter and space, of change and of life, we carry with us today an image of the giant machine as a sign of what the world is really like.

But this world disappeared. In his *Out of My Later Years*,[2] Einstein wrote:

> For several decades most physicists clung to the conviction that a mechanical substructure would be found for Maxwell's theory. But the unsatisfactory results of their efforts led to gradual acceptance of the new field concepts as irreducible fundamentals—in other words, physicists resigned themselves to giving up the idea of a mechanical foundation.

The belief in determinism also declined. Erwin Schrödinger deals with this in his "What Is a Law of Nature?" "Whence arises the widespread belief that the behaviour of molecules is determined by absolute causality, whence the conviction that the opposite is unthinkable? Simply, the custom inherited through thousands of years of thinking causally, makes the idea of undetermined events . . . complete nonsense, a logical absurdity." He further

[1] Simon and Schuster (New York), 1954, p. 126.
[2] Greenwood Press (Westport, Conn.), 1950, p. 179.

states that this way of thinking came about after "observing for hundreds and thousands of years precisely those regularities in the natural course of events, which in the light of our present knowledge are most certainly not governed by causality."

The assumption of laws of nature was based on a most obvious repetitiveness of events. The whole Newtonian world view dealt only with what our senses could observe and with what could be brought into a scientific system of thoughts.

As far as economic laws are concerned, the important feature to notice is that no repetitiveness exists on which the concept of economic laws can be based. However, economic laws are accepted a priori, because it seemed to the founders of economic thinking to be "complete nonsense, a logical absurdity" to assume that any scientists would accept the notion of undetermined events.

Modern physics began to deny the principle of the uniformity of nature, according to which like causes produce like effects, with the emergence of quantum theory. This great change of thinking came about following the findings of Michael Faraday, James Maxwell, and Heinrich Rudolf Hertz. The Newtonian principle of actions at a distance, the basis of the mechanistic world view, could not offer an adequate interpretation for phenomena connected with the electromagnetic field. Actions at a distance were replaced by fields, including that of gravitation. Gravitation was no longer regarded as a mechanical force, but as a mathematical formula governing the curvature of space and the acceleration of moving bodies. Matter and energy ceased to be the basic data of intuition. Space came to be seen as having not an objective reality but rather an order of objects. Nor was time regarded as having any objective reality apart from the order of events by which we measure it.

Max Planck's discovery, at the beginning of our century,

that energy is emitted in discontinuous packets or quanta, led to Niels Bohr's atomic theory, which provided the basis of the hypothesis of indeterminism in nature. Werner Heisenberg's principle of uncertainty, or indeterminacy, has been further developed by the discovery that the prerequisite of classical physics, i.e., the simultaneous knowledge of position and velocity, was impossible. The more accurately we measure the one, the less accurately we are able to define the other. Consequently, we are not able to test the existence of rigorous causal connections.

While the Newtonian world view was based on the conception that nature was an independent reality, observable without reference to the observer and the means of observation, the new view is that we cannot observe nature without disturbing it. Bohr formulated it in a figure showing that man is at once an actor and a spectator in the drama of existence. But in economics, where man as actor is so obvious, we find that economics regards him only as an observer; for him, the system is devoid of all purpose and has to be studied as an objective and determined phenomenon.

The above paragraphs have shown how the Newtonian way of thinking has changed over the past hundred years, despite the fact that the basic content of physics did not change. New views, new concepts, and new methods have been introduced and have established the theoretical basis for our age of electronics, automation, and atomization. But the economic frames of reference have not changed with the times.

We need only take any economics textbook to show that the methodology of physics is, in fact, still applied to economics. We find an endless number of laws, equations, and curves expressing the view that economy is a giant machine in which it is possible to isolate the components and bring them into causal relationships. We must realize that it was a fallacy to accept the methods of thinking and findings derived from the study of nature and apply them to the study of the economy. It would be just as fallacious to apply the findings of economics to modern physics.

THE QUEEN OF ECONOMIC LAWS

No doubt the most popular and generally recognized law, the mother of the "invisible hand," is the law of supply and demand. This law states that the relationship between the supply of commodities and services on the one hand, and the demand for those commodities and services on the other, determines prices—or that the prices determine supply and demand. The higher the prices, the smaller the demanded quantity will be. Perhaps the reason this law is so generally accepted is because it is so readily observable in day to day living.

But the concepts are really deceiving. The laws of supply and demand portray the economy as a mechanism governed by objective laws of absolute value. Consequently, there is no space for our human and subjective values. The use of the term "laws" in conventional economic doctrines serves as a justification for the value-free or value-neutral economics that we now have. Thus, the thinking human being acts only as an outside observer of the system in a relationship similar to that of the astronomer viewing the stars.

It is not of importance whether we speak of economics in terms of laws or not. What is crucial is that we attempt to describe our economy realistically. Conventional economic theory is not leading us toward reality, but further away from it. It is reducing an economic system of thinking subjects to a system of equations, to a branch of mathematics. The concept of the law of supply and demand, like any economic law, is a demonstration of the attempt to push into the background the active role of man and his contribution to the development of and his intellectual impact on the economic system.

Any man with common sense may be surprised to learn that the relationship between supply and demand has to do with an economic law. The average consumer most likely acts according to common sense: in the case of higher prices, he just cannot afford to buy as much as he could when prices were lower. If he lost his ability to think, he would probably spend all his money without looking at prices. He acts economically only due to the fact that he does think and is thus able to formulate his interests. He would hardly understand that he is acting according to some universal law in which people react in definite and impersonal ways to fluctuating prices. It would seem even more mysterious to him that when the relationship between the quantity of goods and the purchasing power changes, the prices will also change. He may know that if the temperature on a closed vessel is increased, the pressure will rise, but he would probably be surprised to learn that the same mechanical reaction is found in the economy.

At this stage, we are not concerned with whether a relationship exists between price and supply or price and demand. What should be questioned is the mechanistic interpretation of this relationship. Let us look at the market, for example, to see the fallacy of this approach. In order to see the phenomena more clearly, let it be a perfect market, as it existed in the "good old days," when the consumers met the producers at the market place.

THE MARKET

Consumers and producers entered the market arena as militant opponents. The consumers tried to buy at prices as low as possible, and the producers tried to sell at prices as high as possible. The market was a conflict situation of thinking people, each interested in his own advantage, and each trying to make use of any weak point of his opponents. When the consumer guessed that there was a low demand as compared with the supply, he figured that the producer would want to avoid bringing the produced goods home from the market place and would therefore be willing to sell them cheaper. On the other hand, when the producer guessed that there was a greater need than the existing supply was able to meet, he felt sure that the consumer, being in need of the goods, would pay more.

In this situation, it was not the price which determined the demand or supply, nor the converse. Human beings, the actors in the market, thought in terms of their own interests, evaluated the situation as far as the advantages or disadvantages were concerned, and determined each of these categories—the price, the demand, the elasticity of demand and supply. Herein lies the *fallacy with the mechanistic approach.*

The fact that people think is responsible for both repetitive and nonrepetitive behavior. We can predict, to a certain extent, the behavior of a group of people in a given situation based on the fact that they will tend to behave in the same way as they did in a similar situation in the past. However, it is also possible that they will behave differently. Applied to economics, this means that a shift in prices may or may not influence people to change their demand. We should also be aware that prices do not rise or fall by themselves. Here again, thinking and acting man is responsible.

Classical economic theory was formulated on the basis of the development of the society at that time. The market of this society was a meeting place for producers and consumers. Generally speaking, the market place consisted of the same people, and their reactions were relatively stable. This stability in conditions, mind, and, consequently, actions reflected an age of relatively small changes. The economy was based mainly on empirical thinking which is, by its very nature, a slow process.

This means that as long as the level of thinking on which the economic process is based is relatively stable, it seems that we may predict or discover a "law" according to which people act in a repetitive way. But once this stage has been transcended, and science is being applied to the economy, the level of thinking, and, consequently, the whole economy becomes dynamic. This dynamism is not lawful. It is instead a reflection of how the minds of people apply science and react.

The basic differences between the less developed societies and modern markets are not difficult to see. In the modern markets, we do not find consumers and producers, but mainly consumers and distributors, with the big producer corporations behind the scenes. No longer do we have a situation where the consumer and producer confront each other to determine the prices; prices are determined long before the commodity ever reaches the market.

One of the outstanding features of the market is its development from the simple classical market into a number of different and interrelated markets. Even if a situation occurs in which the producer of a particular product actually confronts the consumer in the market, he is very likely subject to the developments of other markets. No longer is he master of his production. He has to function within an integrated system which includes the stock market of investors, the financial market including the stock market, the raw material markets where producers meet, the real estate market, and many others. The autonomous functioning of individual markets that occurred in the classical market no longer takes place. Rather, there exists a close interaction of numerous markets, which, in many cases, combine to control the producers themselves.

Let us consider an example which shows just how far removed man's role in determining prices is from the supply and demand relationship. If a car factory releases a number of its workers, we obviously have an increased supply of workers. According to the law of supply and demand, the cost of labor should be cheaper. But because labor is organized, even with this increase in unemployment, we could still face an increase in wages. As the prices of cars are determined by wages and profit, the increase in salaries would cause the prices to rise. Here is a prime example of the price of cars having little, if any, relationship to the supply of and demand for cars.

Labor organized itself and became conscious of its role in the market. This market, as any other market, is a confrontation of diverse interest groups. In order to be as strong as possible, or as strong as the powerful corporations, labor created well-organized, militant associations. It is the trade unions and the corporations who, directly or indirectly, fix the prices of all commodities by fixing the prices of rewards. The consumer only has the choice of "take it or leave it." The situation in the labor market is a most demonstrative proof that prices, as well as any other economic category, are basically the result of our ability to think and to act accordingly.

THE CONCEPT OF DIMINISHING RETURNS

The law of diminishing returns also demonstrates this systematic elimination of the role of man's ability to think. This law states that an increase in some outputs relative to other fixed inputs will, in a given technology, cause total output to increase; after a point, however, the extra output resulting from the same additions of extra input is likely to be less and less. To exemplify this law, we read in textbooks that, given a certain amount of land, we cannot employ any number of workers and expect that each additional worker will increase the output by the same amount. This is, of course, a truism. We would hardly find a farmer who would employ more workers or use more fertilizers than necessary if he had any common sense at all.

The more developed an economy or a production process is, the more complicated a task it becomes to optimize or maximize the difference between input and output. Bad marketing, bad design, bad engineering, or bad management will bring a diminishing return, although in none of these cases have "additions or extra inputs" been applied.

The law of diminishing returns is a demonstration of how economic performance is explained by avoiding its essence. It teaches us to see only the quantitative side, that more workers and more capital have been used. If we see a growing return, we simply state that the capital input has increased the productivity.

How can we express diminishing return in terms of mechanistic and quantifiable laws once we realize that *the real reasons for a diminishing return are errors in the realm of thinking, judgment, and expectation?* The development of economy since the time of the classics is proof alone that the intellectual level on which production, administration, banking, transportation, and management, etc., are based has increased. It is frightening to observe how a most sophisticated discipline like economics has developed its sophistication by neglecting the role of thinking in its subject matter, and how much thought is still being devoted to neglecting the role of the brain in economy.

THE FALLACY
OF EQUILIBRIUM

According to the laws of thermodynamics, if we have hot air in one place and cold air in another, then equilibrium must occur. The hot air could be considered as "upward sloping," the cold air as "downward sloping," and at their intersection is the natural and stable state of affairs. This same principle of equilibrium is applied to economics. If we combine the downward sloping demand curve and the upward sloping supply curve, an intersection results which is the equilibrium price.

This is logical if we are considering a few commodities offered in a primitive market in which the producers and consumers met. There, the producers worked in a market they knew and performed as sellers, and the consumers knew the scope of the supply offered. But if we compare contemporary market economy to a very underdeveloped one like that at the time of Smith and Marx, this concept of equilibrium becomes meaningless and even misleading.

Our economy consists of a great number of markets and

types of goods produced. Each kind of production has its own dynamism of productivity. Upon understanding the complex nature of our market system and how prices are actually determined, we can only conclude that now it is *disequilibrium* which is the typical state of affairs. In any developed economy, *there is not even a tendency toward equilibrium. Disequilibrium is the normal state; equilibrium is the anomaly.*

In economic theory, equilibrium is achieved by shifting the *demand or supply curve*. With what we have concluded thus far, it is obvious that present economics is far more concerned with the motions of curves than with the motion of the economy. If we want to achieve equilibrium, we cannot rely on an "invisible hand" or any other market mechanism. We have to interfere with the economy by introducing an organ, a "visible hand," into the system which will *create* an equilibrium in which the economy performs at full capacity and meets the needs and demands of the consumer. The government, in acting as this organ, would become a subsystem of the whole socioeconomic system. Its task would be to take all the measures necessary to bring the supply and demand relationship into at least asymptotic equilibrium.

The most outstanding characteristics of disequilibrium are unemployment and unstable prices. The answer to these cannot be found in economic laws. It is the task of the "visible hand," the government, to create an economy with full employment and stable prices.

If we believe that equilibrium is the natural state of affairs, then we end up developing more sophisticated theories and simpler measures to eliminate the disequilibrium. Economists have long assumed that such action as a mere increase in money supply or a tuning between monetary and fiscal policy would prove effective. As we can see from our present economic state, the result of these assumptions tends to deepen the disequilibrium to a state of depression. On the other hand, if we view disequilibrium as the natural state of affairs, then we will be able to look for perhaps simpler *theories*—and more sophisticated measures.

PART 3

THE TWO ECONOMIC REVOLUTIONS

THE PLANNED ECONOMY

Planned economy is more than just the result of the revolution in Russia in 1917; it represents a revolutionary attempt at making man able to control his economy. Great hopes and expectations followed this first attempt to plan an economy, especially in light of the deep depression that endangered the very foundations of Europe and America at that time. Half a century has passed since the idea of planning an economy became a reality in Russia, and during that time, their concepts have been introduced in a number of countries.

Their type of planning is referred to as the Soviet model. This model is characteristically comprehensive. It includes not only the planning of the whole economic process but also its infrastructure, such as education and science. All enterprises receive their target figures from a central planning body through their respective ministries. The target figures, which are absolutely binding, refer to the materials produced, services, finances, and number of employees, as well as to the total sum and structure of wages each enterprise has at its disposal.

It is not our intention here to become involved in the details of planning. Different forms of planning have been introduced, but the Soviet model is the only one that involves the whole socioeconomic system. Other types were mere attempts to introduce some elements of planning into a basically nonplanned economy. We will deal, therefore, only with Soviet planning—and all the more so because the Soviet model is being applied to over one-third of the world's population, including that of the People's Republic of China.

We can make two important observations about the experiences of the planned economies. First, they have demonstrated that it is possible to formulate socioeconomic objectives for an economy based on applied science and to break these objectives down into target figures for every aspect of production. This proved to be possible even before having the benefit of computers. Planners succeeded in establishing target figures for the production of every major commodity and service, for maintaining full employment, increasing the standard of living, avoiding inflation, and many other goals. Their success in formulating such plans is proof that it is possible to use available statistics, factual material, and knowledge of the main trends of the development of science and technology to formulate the goal to be achieved.

The second observation that we can make about planned economies is that their plans never work. On the surface, there seems to be nothing more rational than to organize the economy according to a plan that integrates the activities of countless enterprises into a single enterprise, which works without waste, produces for a planned market, and merges all aspects of production into one perfect and predictable machine. Why, then, in nearly fifty years of planning in the U.S.S.R., has no plan ever been fulfilled? In countries at varying stages of development, this type of planning has been introduced. Even in cases where the target figures have been reached, the plans have always failed. From these failures, we have no choice but to conclude that, despite its logic, planning is somehow not rational in practice. How can we explain the fact that, for instance, Soviet planned agriculture employs seven to eight times as many workers as American agriculture, but still produces less? Why is it that the output per capita per unit investment is so much lower in Czechoslovakia's planned economy than it is in Austria, where economy is not planned, despite the fact that these two countries were on a par before planning was introduced in Czechoslovakia?

It would be an oversimplification to blame the failures of planning on bad planning methods or on the errors of individual planners. Although planned economies have suffered from these shortcomings, this is not any more significant in explaining the failure of planning than any other peripheral factors of the economy.

The real reason that planning, despite its logic, is inefficient will be apparent only if we approach planning from a different angle. We can begin by observing that, as long as an economy is underdeveloped, planning and centralization of management may be rational and can be efficient. For example, it may be very practical to allocate resources through some plan that is oriented toward the greatest possible growth, since, at that stage, the problem of economic growth is the primary one. It is also true that at this stage of development the number of people who have skills capable of running an economy is very limited. In this light, it would be rational to concentrate them into one centralized planning body and give them the responsibility for running the whole economy instead of reducing their effectiveness by dispersing them into hundreds of enterprises.

But in developed economies, there is a qualitatively different problem. All of the target figures issued by the planning body, which were reasonable and rational in an underdeveloped economy, reverse themselves. In developed economies, with their large and complex corporations, individual enterprises can function efficiently only accordingly to their own interests and levels of performance, and these are different from those of the macrosphere. When an economy is underdeveloped, the performance level of the macrosphere (the economy as a whole) and that of the microsphere (the economy on the level of individual enterprises), while not identical, are not significantly different. In a highly developed economy, however, each enterprise is based on applied science and is a system of its own. The macrosphere is concerned with the results of the efforts of the whole sphere of enterprises. As a result, there is a permanent conflict situation between the micro- and the macrospheres.

As the labor force is limited, the interest of the macrosphere is for each enterprise to employ as few workers as possible. The enterprises, however, are interested in employing extra workers with which to fill vacancies and to fulfill their plans easily. In addition, they do not have to be concerned with paying for extra workers, as the cost is financed by the planning body. This type of contradiction has a tremendous effect in a planned economy: If the "inflated" demands for employees of an enterprise are met by the planning body, the consequence is an overstaffing of that enterprise and a shortage of workers in others.

The interest of the planning body is to have full employment based on making full use of the capacity of the existing working power, whereas the concern of the enterprise is to have a certain reserve army of workers without increasing its production target figures. These two interests concur only exceptionally. In practice, they create what is called in the terminology of a planned economy "disproportions," the most typical feature of planned economy.

We face the same kind of conflict situation in price and unit fixing. When the plan's target figures are expressed in monetary units, it is in the interests of an enterprise to produce goods that are high priced rather than low priced. In such a case, it would obviously be easier to fulfill the target with expensive goods than with cheap ones. If the target figures were to be expressed in units of product, the enterprise would be interested in reaching those figures with commodities which they find easiest to produce. For instance, in the steel industry, a plant would prefer to produce thick sheets of steel rather than thin ones (to fulfill the target figures with the thick ones is much easier), regardless of the needs of the economy. If the steel industry produces thick sheets, all of the equipment and machinery made from this steel will be heavier and could be less efficient. This kind of inefficiency could be detrimental to the economy as a whole, for, most likely, other industries determine their figures based on a certain quality of steel.

In the light of this situation, it is possible to understand how the plan may have been fulfilled and the target figures may have been reached without fulfilling the larger economic requirements of the plan. In the case of both price fixing and unit fixing, the interests of the microsphere are in direct conflict with the interests of the macrosphere. These contradicting interests are an intrinsic feature, and one source of the failure, of planning.

A further source of the inefficiency of planned economies is related to the fact that in most cases target figures express quantity, whereas qualitative aspects cannot be, as a rule, expressed in target figures. Consequently, to fulfill a plan that demands quantity, the concern for quality is pushed into the background. Because they must concentrate on the target figure, the primary concern of both management and labor is quantity rather than quality. In such a system, a concern for the quality of the goods being produced is neither logical nor practical. There is no room for the kind of thinking that might favor fewer goods of higher quality, as this would result in a failure to fulfill the plan. Thus, an orientation toward target figures forces the enterprise to produce as many commodities as demanded by the plan, no matter how low the quality.

In an enterprise based on applied science, i.e., on a high level of thinking, a subtle pressure to think in terms of quantity alone (and in the planned economies, this pressure is anything but subtle) can be extremely detrimental. An orientation toward thinking in mere quantitative categories has created a situation in the East where maximum wages are planned, as distinct from the situation in the West, where labor pressure has led to legal limits on minimum wages. Wages and salaries are dictated not by ability, but by the plan. The resulting egalitarianism discourages initiative and ability. It eliminates any stimulus for an individual worker to go beyond the limited space for rational or creative thinking that is alloted to him by the plan. It is possible for a worker to earn more, but to do so, he must produce more in a situation where increased production leads to decreased quality.

Another problem of planning arises from the desire of each enterprise to have the lowest possible target figures. If an enterprise's target is low, it can more easily be reached. If it is reached, the management of the enterprise will be rewarded for having fulfilled the target set for them. If the target is not met, sanctions are used to punish the management for its failure. It is therefore in the interest of the management to hide capacities and to persuade the planning body that it is impossible to fulfill the prevailing target figures. Success in obtaining the lowest possible target figures is the sign of a good manager in a planned economy. In what amounts to the "survival of the fittest," the quality of a manager is strongly dependent on his ability to obtain for himself the smallest feasible target figures. Each manager aims to simply produce enough to achieve the target and as little above the target as possible.

Just as the plan influences the thinking of the managers in an uneconomic direction, the same is also true of its impact on the application of technology. Technical innovations always involve certain risks, especially when methodology is a part of a long-term plan. Once a certain mode of production has been established, it becomes very difficult to change it. (For years, the automobile industry in the East used outdated methods to produce the same cars year after year. Only through the import of whole factories under license from firms in the West have planned economies overcome this inherent retarding tendency.)

It is only in the fields of war production and space production that the Soviets are equal to the Americans, but it is significant that in these two fields there is no central planning. More precisely, the scientists, engineers, and managers in these industries have a free hand to devise their own methods for production and can dictate to the planning body how they will produce and what materials they will need. If the planned task is to reach the moon, they are free to work out whatever plans are necessary to reach this goal. In these areas, the scientists have freedom equal to, and possibly even greater than, the scientists in the United States, with the same or better working conditions. Despite their importance in national defense and the secrecy involved, there are much smaller political demands on these experts than, for instance, those in the textile industry. For the war industries, a man's expertise is the decisive factor in his assignment to a particular position. It is in the consumer industries that expertise is ignored for political considerations, and the resulting economic inefficiency is paid for by the nation's consumers.

Another source of the inefficiency of planned economies can be found in the power exercised by the state apparatus

in controlling the economy. Once the state takes responsibility for the management of all the means of production,
once the state becomes the sole employer, the dependence
of each citizen on the favorable actions of its hierarchic
structure is immense. There is a tremendous pressure on everyone working in an enterprise to conform, not to be "unreasonable." Being reasonable is regarded as recognizing
and abiding by all requirements with no thought that the requirements themselves might be unreasonable. Absurdities
in the system can persist for long periods of time, or at least
until they come to the attention of the leadership of the planning body. All of this is underlined by the role of the party.
The state apparatus is, after all, an operative organ of the
party and it freely makes use of its right to interfere with
enterprises, management, and personnel. Obedience and
conformity pervade the system; the enterprise is obedient to
the state apparatus and to the corresponding organ of the
party, whether it is a factory party organization, local party
organization, or ultimately, the central committee. As a result, the whole economy is squeezed into channels where intellectual activity is not encouraged, and where no space is
provided for the individuals to fulfill their own interests. The
consequence is a pan-bureaucratic system.

The absolute bureaucratization of planned economies is
only partly a tendency of big enterprises. This tendency also
exists in the Western counterpart to the big enterprises.
While in the West it may become a source of criticism, in
the planned economies, bureaucratization is not only reinforced by planning, but is the means on which planning is
based.

But the fundamental failure of planning is to be seen in
the fact that it does not recognize brain work as the decisive
factor in modern economy. By this we do not mean that the
East ignores science or technology, nor do we mean that the
leaders in the East are not aware of the role that science can

play. On the contrary, they strongly support scientific ventures, research institutes, and schooling. Despite their subjective esteem for science, it is in the philosophy of economic planning that the role of intellect is ignored.

The planned economies thus embody an irreconcilable contradiction; they represent a modern economy built on a philosophy inadequate for a modern economy. The tragic conflict in Soviet planning lies in the fact that while modern economy is the result of man's creative thinking, the planning of the economic performance negates this very ability of man. Only in the highest echelon of the planned economy, i.e., in the top of the planning body, is creative thinking permitted. The rest of the people must be satisfied with fulfilling administrative target figures. Their intellectual capacity, the real source of wealth, is not being utilized.

This situation has a decisive effect on the intellectual climate within which the economy operates. After fifty years of planning, every member of the economy thinks in terms of target figures. No one would dare take responsibility for something that was not explicitly assigned to him by the target figures. This is the result of the rationale and momentum of planned economies in general. To change this type of economy toward a market economy would, first of all, make an issue of the role and power of the Party itself, and then, even if the Party tried to introduce it, it would take decades for the very demanding and complex market economy to be mastered.

The shortcomings of the planning system are generally recognized in the highest echelons of the Soviet Union and other countries following their model. But there is no attempt made to question the basics of planning. Their answer to the failures is to improve the method of planning and make use of the possibilities of greater efficiency that computerization offers. The recent decision to introduce computerization at the basis of planning will result in more target figures and even less space for creative possibilities. It is not difficult to predict that an absolute computerization will create an absolute technocratic system, the materialization of the Brave New World. It will consequently be the computer programmer who will rule man and society more than any dictator would be able to do. To the advocates of convergence or technocracy in the West, and to those who advocate planning as the solution of our problems, the lessons of more than fifty years of planning should be a warning.

It is particularly important to bear in mind that, apart from economic inefficiency, planning has its impact on the role of man in society. Planning means that the body in power has the right to decide what is to be produced and, consequently, what is to be consumed. Planning cannot involve just the planning of materials and energy; it necessitates that man, too, must become an object of planning. In this sense, planning leads to the neglect of man, his rights, his freedom, even his uniqueness. The great revolutionary idea that planning would free man and make the economy a solid, reliable basis for progress turned into a counterrevolution. Man became, instead of a beneficiary an object of planning; instead of controlling the economy, he is being controlled.

THE KEYNESIAN REVOLUTION

According to the philosophies of the classics, the inherent forces of the laissez faire economy would secure a general equilibrium (which includes an equilibrium between the supply and demand of labor, i.e., full employment). This was to be accomplished in the self-recuperative manner which is intrinsic to a laissez faire economy, as well as by the plethora of economic laws.

The crises of the thirties brought on a great depression for much of the world. It provided the most manifest proof that the expectations of the classics on the "invisible hand" and on economic laws were not valid, and that these basic assumptions of the classics were fallacies. This depression resulted in a great and lasting rate of unemployment and, particularly in Europe, had a considerable impact on the whole political development. It provided one of the factors that led to the emergence of Nazism in Germany and, at the other end of the spectrum, to the strengthening of the Communist Party. More and more, the difficult times impressed upon the masses the outdated nature of liberal capitalism with its democratic form, suggesting Stalinism and Nazism as the only viable alternatives to the existing system. Stalinism was viewed favorably because the Soviet Union was not burdened with the problem of unemployment; Hitler's appeal was that he promised an end to Germany's unemployment.

Soon after Hitler came to power, his Minister of the Economy, Hjalmer Schacht, throwing overboard the teaching of the classics, introduced "government spending" in preparation for the war, thereby eliminating unemployment in Germany. In the Soviet Union, government spending "had taken place since the revolution." Due to the fact that the government owned all means of production, it provided the necessary money supply.

It is in this context that we should understand Keynesian theory, which presented to classical economics the concept of government spending to eliminate unemployment and save democracy. John Maynard Keynes actually saved the philosophy of the classics, the philosophy of liberalism. He explained government spending by contending not that these philosophies had failed, but that there were reasons which justified the interference of a democratic government into those fields where the "invisible hand" had failed to act.

According to the philosophy of the classics, all savings were transformed into investment, implying that savings had to equal investment. If a farmer, for example, saved, he did so in order to invest later and consequently improve his productive capacity. Businesses followed the same pattern. On this assumption, the classics were, according to Keynes, correct. Keynes accepted that with the equating of these two factors, a disequilibrium could not occur. But what if the people who saved and those who invested were different? What would insure the equating of these factors? Keynes pointed out that the great majority of savings was provided by households. He also cited that households were highly subjective entities influenced primarily by personal and unpredictable motivations. These subjective values Keynes discussed in terms of propensities to save, to consume, and to hoard.

On the other hand, corporations have to draw from households for investment. But the motivations and interests of investors are very different from those of the household. While individual household savings are dependent on the subjective values of the individuals, investments can be, and usually are, dependent on another range of dynamic and relatively unpredictable elements in the economic system. In fact, according to the Keynesian school, these elements often come from "outside the system itself" (technology, politics, expectations, confidence, etc.). Therefore, owing to the fact that some people save and others invest, and that the motivations for both differ, it is highly unlikely that savings and investment will equal each other automatically. We see a kind of "anomaly" where economic forces do not equate savings and investment, and this is the cause of unemployment. It is precisely here that Keynes believed that government must interfere.

To avoid such a disequilibrium, Keynes suggested that the government pour money into the economy. His famous example reads like this: "If the treasury were to fill old bottles with old bank notes, bury them at suitable depths in disused coal mines which are then filled up to the surface with town rubbish, and leave it to the private enterprise on well-tried principles of laissez faire to dig the notes up, we could eliminate unemployment." Keynes did not actually advise this as the main remedy, as he hoped there would be more sensible ways for the government to spend money. But in his view, it would have been better than nothing and would have contributed to solving the problem of unemployment.

We can see how, on the one hand, Keynes justified the philosophy of the classics and the socioeconomic system that was based on this philosophy, while, on the other hand, he introduced two elements which were in absolute contradiction to the classics' whole system of thinking and, in a way, contrary to economic thinking as a whole. One element was the principle of spending money for noneconomic purposes, spending for the sake of creating equilibrium, even if applied in such a manner as in the case of "the bottle." We remember that the basic assumption of the classics was that every actor in the economy will act from selfish economic motivations. Thrift, economizing, became a universal economic principle. Into this system of thought, Keynes introduced spending for noneconomic purposes. Spending thus became an end in itself, and considerations other than economic ones entered into economic thinking.

But as spending for noneconomic purposes by the government has to be projected in the form of taxes, thus raising prices, the door to inflation was consequently opened. Keynesian theory, then, is basically a rationale for inflation. It is a matter of fact that the history of the economy for the last few decades has been a history both of growing Keynesian influence and of inflation.

The second contradicting element, which actually negated the basic principles of the classics, was the new role of the government. The government should no longer be an external factor that does not interfere with the economy. In other words, the economy cannot rely on the functioning of the invisible hand; it needs the government to be a part of the economic system.

Although Keynes was contradicting the self-recuperative power assumed by the classics (and, subsequently, their basic philosophy), he did not completely deny its functioning. In order to save the classics and the economic philosophy on which democracies were based, he declared that classical equilibrium was a "special case." Keynes formulated a "general theory" which encompassed the self-recuperative power of a laissez faire economy, but acknowledged that a disequilibrium could occur in the form of unemployment.

In order to ascertain the validity of the essence of Keynes's theory, let us deal with his basic assumption that unemployment results from a mismatching of savings and investments, and that, through government spending bridging this gap, classical equilibrium would be the general rule. Let us suppose that savings equal investments. In order to make the example clearer, we might even assume that households spend everything they earn, meaning that savings are zero. The corporations, on the other hand, are only replacing worn out machinery, i.e., net investment would also be zero. A case of classic equilibrium should take place. But is this what would actually occur?

We have to assume that the replaced machinery would be more efficient, and that higher levels of design, of organization of labor, and of management would be applied. We would see under such conditions that the same input has resulted in a higher output. But is it really the same input? The quantifiable part of the input, that which can be expressed in monetary units, would remain the same. But we should also be aware that the most important input, that which cannot be quantified and that which conventional economics does not embody in its theories, is the intellectual input. It is not investment, but the higher intellectual level on which the economic process is based, that increases the output. Investment could even be a source of economic decline if the intellectual level on which it is based is low.

As the level of thinking in both technology and management is dynamic, it provokes a dynamism in production. Unemployment, the disequilibrium in the labor market, should be seen as the result of the dynamism of production not being equaled by an adequate dynamism of consumption. Consequently, instead of assuming that an equilibrium between savings and investment is the central issue, we should concern ourselves with developing a mechanism which would equate the dynamism of production with that of consumption.

At the time of the classics of capitalism and socialism, the application of science to the economy existed in only rudimentary form. Consequently, there existed a lack of understanding of the role of the thinking man as the basis of the economy. But by Keynes's time, the application of science had become the most outstanding feature of developed economies. Even without savings, the economy became dynamic and grew because of the intellectual level on which it was based. In this historical context, then, savings lost its original role. Now, for example, if savings are turned into investments, the rate of economic growth may increase, but not the dynamism of consumption because more savings mean less consumption. Therefore, savings increase the disparity between the dynamism of production and the dynamism of consumption. Keynes's theory does not incorporate this dimension.

We must remember in looking at Keynes's concern with unemployment that it was dictated by political motivation. He saw the danger of the "complete collapse of the financial structure of modern capitalism." Keynes's great contribution was that he found a new tool for dealing with economics. The interference of the government in the economy opened a new avenue. But the justification of noneconomic spending has turned the Keynesian revolution against its very aims. The economy, as developed under the impact of this philosophy, has brought about a combination of inflation and unemployment, which endanger our civilization as much as unemployment alone did in the thirties.

As we mentioned earlier, the first revolution, that of planning, turned into its opposite. The government was seen as an external factor acting as the owner of the system. Consequently, the main emphasis on the design of the future was the interest of the government in maintaining its power over society and its economy. The objective of the Keynesian revolution was to eliminate a depression manifesting itself in massive unemployment. As unemployment was perceived as more of a political than an economic problem, any price was to be paid for its solution, regardless of the effect on the economy. In the cases of both of these revolutions, economics played only a secondary role of importance next to political considerations.

We should realize that both of these revolutions were revolutions in name only. They did not center on the understanding that the mature economy would develop into an integrated system. They did not concern themselves with the efficient performance of this system, the interests of the consumer, full employment, and stable prices. No solution which fails to deal with all of these areas deserves to be called a revolution.

PART 4

THE MACROORGAN
AND ITS TOOLS

THE MONEY SUPPLY

We have mentioned that disequilibrium is a feature of every mature economy. The assumption that equilibrium can result from a self-recuperative power in the economy has proven to be fallacious. It is the macroorgan, the government, which is needed to fulfill the task of creating this equilibrium.

The government's approach to creating equilibrium should not interfere with the performance of the enterprises, however. Still, to run a corporation efficiently requires a high level of managerial skill. Once the freedom for its application is limited, the functioning of the corporation is seriously affected. However, as we have shown with the Soviet planned economy, direct interference into enterprise performance causes inefficiency, and the consumer, in the end, pays the price for it. As the economy is not merely the sum of its components, but a system with its own interests, dynamism, and performance level, we should see the causes of disequilibrium first of all as a manifestation of the behavior of the system.

The relationship between the system and its components is paradoxical. Even if all the components operate competently, it does not mean that the system as a whole is functioning efficiently; unemployment and inflation can exist despite the best performance of the components. (On the other hand, if the components are not acting efficiently, neither will the whole system.) More often than not, though, unemployment, inflation, and economic uncertainty tend to create conditions that inhibit the normal and competent functioning of enterprises by forcing them to adapt to the dysfunctioning of the system.

The role of the government in influencing the performance of the economy, then, should be two-fold. First, it must offer optimal conditions for each enterprise to function at its highest level of performance and according to its own interests. Second, the government has to orient the system toward an objective, such as full employment and a stable price level. In order to fulfill such a task, the government will need tools. Obviously, these tools will have to be ones which are beyond the scope of the enterprise level and belong only to the macroorgan. One such tool is the money supply.

Originally, money used to be a creation of individual actors in the form of commodity-money. The growing sophistication in production and in the economy led to more intensive economic interaction and to the use of precious metals, which were, in actuality, still a commodity-money. In the eighteenth century, fiat money was introduced. Although it had no inherent commodity value, it was backed by governments and banks which had precious metals and other assets at their disposal.

At this stage, though, money and the money supply had not yet essentially changed. First of all, money supply was still not a macroeconomic category, as businesses were able to create the necessary supply of money. Second, throughout its history, money retained its three basic functions as a medium of exchange, a store of value, and a standard of value. While monetary theories today still regard these three as the basic functions of money in a modern economy, they are actually no longer primary functions.

In an age of permanent inflation, money ceases to be a standard of value. Its basic function as a store of value is also not the same as it once was. We are seeing a growing tendency to exchange money for more reliable stores of value such as real estate, art objects, etc. Even its function as a medium of exchange has fundamentally changed. Economic growth imposed upon money a new primary function, that of a catalyst. (By catalyst, we mean that money is now a *necessary* agent for triggering and maintaining economic processes.) This is not to say that money has not always acted as a catalyst. Rather, those qualities that used to be basic to money are now peripheral, whereas the catalytic function of money in a mature economy has become its most outstanding characteristic.

Owing to this faculty of money, the scope of the money supply has a tremendous impact on the functioning of the economy. Without a sufficient money supply, the performance of the economy is undermined and cannot reach its full potential. Money supply has consequently become a crucial economic problem, in both theory and in practice. It raises the fundamental question of who is to bear the responsibility for determining the supply of money. Before Keynes, it was assumed that the self-recuperative power of the economy would take care of the money supply. Actually, during this time the enterprises bore the responsibility for creating money, as the government offered only a fraction of the supply needed for a performing economy.

Keynes's great contribution was to speak out in favor of

the government's supplying the economy with money if the microsphere was not able to do it. The government could even, as we have learned, spend money for no reasonable purpose at all, just as long as it was pouring money into the economy. Based on this perspective, far more sophisticated methods were invented for regulating the money supply, such as open market regulations, treasury notes, and changing interest (i.e., discount) rates.

We must realize, however, that Keynes's theories did not institute the necessary significant change in the responsibility for the money supply. To a very great extent, the money supply still rests with the enterprises and the households. Measures such as changing interest rates and open market regulations still are interdependent with propensities to save and to consume, with expectations, and with other subjective reactions of economic agents. As long as the government depends on such factors, it can never bear the full responsibility for the money supply.

Theories based on Keynes's principles were developed in part to avoid economic collapse. Instead, they have not only contributed to a chaotic situation, they continue to perpetuate it. By being dependent on enterprises for the money supply, the government is forced to interfere with them. Changing interest rates means that the cost of credit is not being determined by the interaction of businesses in the market, but by administrative measures. Tightening the money supply by increasing interest rates makes it impossible for enterprises to utilize their full capacity even if there is a demand. Increased taxes will also bring pressure on businesses not to operate to their full potential. We can only reiterate that the efficient functioning of the enterprises and their resulting important contribution to the growth of the economy is hampered by direct interference by the government.

There is no doubt that the money supply should be

treated as predominantly a macroeconomic category. Therefore, it should be solely the responsibility of the government to supply the economy with as much money as needed.

Let us demonstrate this principle with a simple example. If it becomes possible to control precipitation, the responsibility for its control should necessarily lie with the government. Basically, all the government has to do is to guarantee that the needed amount of rain will always be available. What is grown should remain the responsibility of the farmers. Allowing individuals to control precipitation would create a chaotic situation analogous to letting businesses and households be responsible for the supply of money.

In this respect, precipitation functions as a catalyst. For its effect to be fully appreciated, not only must the necessary amount fall, but it must fall at the proper times and in the right places. Similarly, the government should provide the necessary supply of money when and where it is needed, without interfering with the performance of individual businesses.

It is at this point that the notion of government spending for noneconomic purposes would lose its justification. The concept of *"government spending"* could be replaced by *government lending*. The government would be responsible for providing money by supplying the banks with loans in the form of deposits. As the needed money supply would be deposited by the government, there would not be any reason to encourage rewards for saving, i.e., interest. The economy would therefore no longer be dependent upon savings and deposit-loan ratios for its supply of money. This would also cause a major change in the financial function of banks. They would continue to lend money on strictly commercial considerations without having to rely on deposits from households and corporations. The government would supply all the deposits or any part of them not satisfied by the private sector.

Upon implementing this procedure, there would be no reason to create banking money except in a limited scope. As changes in the money supply could hardly be as elastic as is necessary for the economy, allowing banks to lend up to, say, 10% more money than their deposits amounted to would compensate for any such inelasticity. The first effect of this change would be a lowering of the interest rates down to a level that would cover the costs of the banks, their risks, and their profits. Business enterprises would not be exposed to the constant risks involved in fluctuating interest rates. In the final analysis, as the costs of credit are projected into prices, the consumer, and actually the whole nation, would benefit from less expensive money and consequently lower prices.

If we accept the notion that it is the responsibility of the government, as the economic macroorgan, to provide the economy with the needed money supply, then we would be giving the government a workable tool to mobilize idle areas of the economy, particularly where unemployment is concerned. The government could accomplish this mobilization by earmarking a portion of its deposits for certain regions in branches of the economy where, due to a lack of financial funds, the working capacity is not being made full use of. (We can see the effective use of such a tool in the present crisis of the building industry. There is both a demand for and a supply of housing, but lack of money paired with prohibitive interest rates creates a housing shortage and unemployment.)

A study would be needed, of course, to determine just which regions, branches, and kinds of skills were not functioning at full capacity, and what would be needed to mobilize them. Such a study is a highly complex task, for it demands a level of thinking, knowledge, and method which transcends empirical thinking. Ideally, employment should be productive, should involve a purposeful use of skill and nonskill, and should be meaningful for both the employees and the economy. At the same time, the means of achieving full employment must not be the cause of any other economic malaise, such as inflation. Though there will be varying values and priorities, any attempt at attaining full employment must take into account these fundamental prerequisites. But as this program affects everyone, in the end it should be the people who decide on the priorities to be used. Consequently, alternative programs of full employment should become part of the democratic mechanism—and political democracy be expanded into the field of economy.

This expansion cannot occur, however, by relying upon conventional fiscal and monetary policies as a viable solution. The government should neither act as "the manager of the economy" (as in planned economies), nor be restricted to changing interest rates or changing taxes. These measures leave the roots of our present chaotic situation untouched and merely "heal" a few of the consequences.

In a mature economy, the responsibility of the government does not end with the creation of full employment. One of the fundamental characteristics of our modern economy is that our problems are too large for solutions generated by individual enterprises alone. Problems such as the energy crisis, the scarcity of raw materials, and the ecological problem all need the active assistance of the macroorgan. The solution of these crises are of such vital importance that they cannot be left to accidents in the market.

We are faced with two seemingly contradictory principles. On the one hand, the effect of the performance of the economy depends on the efficient functioning of the enterprises. This functioning should not be undermined by governmental interference. Changing interest rates, tax rates, purchasing power, and a growing number of administrative regulations represent such a direct or indirect interference of the government into the sphere of the enterprises as to make the free enterprise system become an anachronism.

On the other hand, a mature economy needs a macro-organ. Without its active participation, our present disequilibrium will continue to endanger the foundations of the economy. Furthermore, new economic tasks have emerged that transcend the capacity of individual enterprises.

To reconcile both of these principles, we must provide the government with a tool that enables it to fulfill its duties without interfering with the efficiency of the enterprises. Without such a tool, we will not be able to cure the malaise of all mature economies. The money supply (one should actually say the credit supply) is one of these tools.

We must bear in mind, however, that it is not sufficient just to supply the economy with the necessary amount of means of payments and to allocate some portions of it to achieve certain goals. The study of the conditions under which these aims, such as full employment, are to be attained must be a comprehensive one. An understanding of the implications of using a tool for certain goals must take into consideration ecological requirements, new energy resources, and the economizing of raw materials, before the allocation of earmarked credits is implemented.

It is important that this study not only be concerned with the total sum of money or credit supply needed for utilizing the full capacity of the economy, but that it also involve where earmarked deposits should be made available. We would end up with two kinds of government deposits. The first, the obvious majority, would not be earmarked and would be used by the business enterprises without any restriction. The second type of deposit would be assigned to insure that full employment and other desired goals were met.

We should emphasize here that there is more involved in

the supplying of money than just its quantitative aspect. We are also going to have to be concerned with the "quality" of the money, i.e., whether its purchasing power will be stable or whether it will be determined in the enterprise level and consequently be unstable. Without the qualitative, as well as the quantitative, aspects of the money supply emanating from the macrosphere, we will most likely perpetuate our present chaos and face even greater inflation. Once we come to the conclusion that it is the responsibility of the government to issue money or credits, it can only be the duty of the government to insure the stability of its purchasing power, as well.

Finally, upon accepting the principle that the government should provide the economy with the needed money or credit supply, we should also look at the government's present means of taking money out of the economy. Just as the government should not interfere with enterprises by not providing a sufficient money supply, it should interfere even less when withdrawing this money for taxation purposes. Thus, before we can deal with the problem of the government in securing a stable price level, we will have to question the concept of taxation.

OUTDATED TAXATION

"The state needs money to pay its bills. It gets its dollars to pay for its expenditures from taxes." However people may grumble over taxes, this philosophy is generally accepted as the most rational justification of taxation. Indeed, could anything be more elementary than the government having to pay its bills?

Before questioning the validity of this philosophy, let us first understand who is actually paying the taxes. While it may be obvious that individuals pay personal income taxes, that corporations pay corporate taxes, and that households pay excise and sales taxes, if we look below the surface, we will find a completely different situation.

A corporation, for example, only technically pays taxes. In reality, they are paid by the consumer, since the taxes are projected into the prices of the commodities. The taxes the corporations do pay to the Internal Revenue Service come from this projection into prices. For instance, the mining industry includes the money it has to pay for taxes in the price of the coal and ore it sells to the steel industry. The steel industry adds costs, profits, and its taxes to the price of the steel sold to the machine tool industry. The process again repeats itself as the equipment is sold to, say, the shoe industry. The shoe factory, in selling its shoes to the wholesale or retail trade, adds to the price, again, the costs of production, profit, and its expected amount of taxes. The wholesale and retail trade, in turn, do the same. In the end, the consumer pays not only for all the costs incurred in the long process of the production of the shoes, but also for the accumulated taxes the preceding agents have included in the price of their product. It is thus the consumer who actually pays the corporate taxes.

It should still be pointed out that a substantial part of prices are the wages paid by industry in the process of production, and not taxes. While wages are also taxed, the income tax is added to the net salary. Therefore, the costs of production can be seen as net wages plus income tax. The prices, however, include gross wages. Thus, in the last instance, the consumer is even paying for the employee's tax. Only as far as excise taxes are concerned does the consumer have no doubt that it is he who actually pays the taxes.

Upon realizing that it is basically the consumer who pays the taxes, let us return to questioning the validity of the philosophy that "the state needs money to pay its bills." All over the world, and even in ancient societies, taxes were collected and paid, either in kind, or in forced labor, gold, or paper money. The rulers needed these kinds of payments to meet their own expenses and to preserve their power structures. In every respect, governments, before the emergence of democracies, were external factors, staying outside and above the people being ruled. In these kinds of societies, it was perfectly valid to say that the rulers "needed money to pay their bills." But even though the power structures and relationships since then have changed, we still apply the same institution of taxation.

Serfdom, the unpaid labor force of peasants, and the forced delivery of tithes were all abolished with the emergence of democratic societies. Yet we still think in terms of the government having bills to pay and the nation having to supply the money to pay the bills.

Once we leave this anachronistic concept of taxation behind us, we see that the government should offer as many means of payment as necessary, both for the needs of the performance of the economy and for the costs incurred in fulfilling other duties entrusted to the government by the nation.

Consequently, we have two kinds of money or credit supplies in the economy. In one role, it functions as a catalyst—without a sufficient amount available, the economy cannot perform to its full capacity. The second kind of supply concerns what the government pours into the economy in the form of expenditures.

In order to fulfill its duties, the government employs a great number of people who could otherwise take part in the production of goods and services. In addition, due to its purchases for defense and other purposes, the government absorbs part of the productive capacity of the nation. In this respect, there is less of the "pie" for the consumers. In addition, everyone who is directly or indirectly employed by the government further uses government expenditures as they become consumers in the market. The resulting effect in the market is purchasing power that is larger than the available supply of goods and services, a situation analogous to issuing more theater tickets than there are seats. Not only would some ticket holders not find seats, but *everyone* who bought a ticket would fear not finding an available seat. The basic property of the tickets thus changes. The tickets cease to have as great a value as their ability to guarantee seats decreases.

This simplified example shows us the nature of the problem involved. In the same way that the superfluous theater tickets would have to be voided, it is necessary to "skim off" the extra money that appears in the market as the consequence of government expenditures. The issue here is not that the government needs the money to pay its bills, but that in paying bills it has thus created a situation where the *superfluous* money supply in the market deprives money of its basic property—having purchasing power. In other words, the government has to skim off a proportion of means of payment in the form of taxation, not because it has to "pay its bills," but because superfluous money is detrimental to the consumer and the economy.

In order to indicate the difference between taxing and skimming, let us project the concept of skimming into economic reality and see what new elements it would create. If the principle of skimming were accepted, all taxes would be abolished. Excise taxes, income taxes, and corporate taxes would not exist any longer. Salaries would be reduced by the amount of taxes paid, i.e., net wages would be paid instead of gross. Wage earners would have the same net salaries they had before these measures. The prices the corporations charge would also be reduced by the amount of taxes previously paid. The result would be that the consumer prices of goods and services would be about 40%–50% cheaper.

But we must remember, at the same time we would face a superfluous money supply. The personal income of the nation would now be 40%–50% higher than the sum total of the prices of the goods and services. This would create a situation similar to the one in which more theater tickets had been issued than were seats available. Thus, the government would have to skim off the very same 40%–50% consisting of superfluous money. It could do so by adding a 40%–50% skimming rate at the last link of the distribution chain, where the households buy commodities and services. As a matter of fact, this skimming-off would have exactly the same form as the sales tax; the consumer would actually see no difference at all. The goods and services would consequently cost as much as they did before the skimming had been applied.

We know that the existing forms of income and corporate taxes, however they may be reformed, open fantastic possibilities for tax loopholes and demand a most costly revenue service. The average consumer is not aware that he pays for both the costs of the revenue service as well as for the loopholes. The revenue service is paid out of the budget, and the budget is met by taxes. More than one billion dollars could be saved by eliminating the auditing of income and corporation taxes. Checking the sales tax is a simple measure. The retailer would collect the skimming rate from the consumer in the same way that he collects excise tax and would send the collected money to the revenue service. Auditing these returns would be simple in comparison to the massive bureaucracy deemed necessary for current income and corporate tax collection.

As far as the loopholes are concerned, the assumed income from taxes currently ends up being less than expected. Consequently, the taxation for the next fiscal year must be increased, taking into consideration that not all the taxes will actually be paid. But more importantly, even with tax loopholes, the taxes have still been calculated into the prices. Although the consumer has paid the corporation's taxes, they are not being sent to their destination. According to the estimates, these loopholes amount to many billions of dollars. If they were to be eliminated, the rate of skimming would be less than the original rate of taxes. In other words, if taxes meant something like 40%–50% of the consumer price, it could be expected that the consumer would pay less in the form of skimming.

In the conventional tax system, the budget is paid for by

the total sum of the taxes. For instance, if the budget is $300 billion, then the government takes this sum in taxes to cover the budget. The principle of skimming, however, is not directly related to the budget. With skimming, the government issues the $300 billion to pay for the budget and then skims off and destroys only the surplus portion of the $300 billion. For example, if the economy is expanding and needs an additional $20 billion, then the government would skim off and shed only $280 billion. Furthermore, owing to a constant expansion of the economy, we can expect that the rate of skimming would always be less than the conventional tax rate.

Each corporation expects a certain profit and assumes that its gross profits will be taxed. This means that any enterprise, in its planning and fixing of prices, figures out its net profit and then adds the tax. Thus, the gross profit is included in the prices. If the expected profit fails to be realized and, instead, the corporation faces a loss, it still collects the taxes calculated in the prices. However, this income is not being passed on to the IRS, but is used toward the losses. The corporation is not paying any taxes, although the consumer who bought the goods paid the amount reserved for taxes.

The principle of skimming, in eliminating corporate taxes, resolves this and similar cases. All that was skimmed off would go directly to the IRS. Although this measure in itself should be a justification for introducing the principle of skimming, the real importance of this principle lies in another field.

We argued that, in the last instance, all taxes are being paid by the consumer. Nevertheless, due to the fact that they are technically paid out of profits by corporations and salaries of income earners, a dependence between high income and government interest is being created. The government and the public at large view high income earners as those who "pay the bill." Therefore, high income earners are treated with careful consideration. It is not the tax-paying consumer, but the corporations and the wealthy who become *personae gratae*. It should be of the utmost importance to make it clear that it is the consumer who pays for all the bills of the nation. The consumer should become conscious of this role.

We should be aware of the fact that the nation actually entrusts its government with certain duties to fulfill, and with paying its bills. Consequently, there should be a kind of contract between the government and its citizens. The government should express in a document what kinds of duties it will fulfill, how much it will spend, and how much it will be necessary to skim off, i.e., to add to the consumer prices. The concept of democracy, then, would not be reduced merely to allowing a nation's citizens the right to elect their representatives in the government. Rather, the right of citizens would be expanded; the budget should be incorporated into the democratic process (a matter we shall deal with in greater detail later), with the same weight political programs or personalities carry. The budget would express the duties of the government, the costs, and the rate of skimming—the contribution of the consumer. Thus, the principle of the rate of skimming is to be seen as one of the bases on which economic democracy could be based.

There is still a further, and no less important, effect of the rate of skimming. It can be realistically assumed that the rate of skimming will move in the neighborhood of 40%–50%. It would be possible to add this 40%–50% to each consumer item, but it would also be possible to break down this rate according to social, cultural, health, educational, and related needs. A low or even a negative rate of skimming could be used for necessities, and luxury goods could be burdened with high rates. Goods and services which are health-oriented could have a far lower rate than those detrimental to health. Cultural products and services could be supported by low or negative rates. Large cars, for example, due to their pollution, could be charged at high rates and small or less-polluting cars at lower rates. Commodities made of recycled material could have preferential rates. The possibilities are endless.

Thus, without direct interferences by bureaucratic measures, the government has an excellent tool for acting in such realms as social justice, the health of the nation, culture, and natural environment. The scope and breakdown of this rate of skimming could also be included in the budget and be incorporated into democratic mechanisms. This would make it possible for the citizen-consumer to have a direct say in how his burden is being used.

We could expect that one of the first reactions to the abandoning of the income tax would be the complaint that it would make "the rich richer and the poor poorer." Such an objection is the expression of a sense of justice, and the obvious concern is that of a just distribution of income. When we abolish taxes, we are eliminating those taxes which are supposed to give the government money to pay its own bills. This does not mean that those with high incomes should remain untouched. They would pay taxes not for the government's use, but for redistribution of income. They would be paying a kind of *social share*. This social share, which would have its own rate on high income levels, would not go toward the conventional budget, but would be used for only certain purposes, such as programs for the benefit of lower income groups. We should be especially cognizant of the fact that the conventional income tax was not meant to redistribute incomes. Conventional income taxes do not provide any benefit for the underprivileged; they are (and have been) used mainly for the purposes that deepen or prolong the tragic fate of these people.

Concerning the redistribution of income, we can derive the following principles. Any personal income share in excess of a certain amount would be burdened with a social share. The social share collected would not go toward the normal budget, but would be collected in a separate account and used for specific purposes. There could be a direct channel, for example, from this account toward housing, health care, social care of the underprivileged, etc. This type of social share, combined with a structured skimming rate, offers a remarkable tool for eliminating a wide field of social injustice.

The elimination of income tax would have a different meaning for enterprises. First, it would deprive the government of the right of interfering with the functioning of the enterprise. Fiscal policy, i.e., the use of taxation as a tool of the government to slow down business activities, is an absurd concept, since here the government is actually preventing the enterprise from increasing the national product.

It is interesting to note that the concept of taxation is taken for granted, that even the most ardent supporters of "free enterprise" do not object to the principle of corporate taxes. There have been many advocates of the view that lowering corporate taxes would have a positive effect on the performance of enterprises. We can imply from this standpoint that the *introduction* of these taxes has had a detrimental effect on enterprises' performance. Therefore, we can see not only how these taxes burden the consumer and decrease business activities, but also how they slow down the growth of the economy which, in turn, lessens the growth of the standard of living of the whole nation.

Another important consequence of eliminating corporate taxes is that it would foster an interest on the part of both the management and the employees to increase the profit. In an economy with a stable price level, an enterprise could not increase profits and rewards by increasing prices, thus further burdening the consumer. The only way to increase profits and rewards would be through increasing the efficiency of the economic performance. The management is always under pressure to be more efficient in its own interest, but now it would have to face the pressure of the employees or their trade unions who see greater efficiency as raising their salaries and their share of the profit. Profit, then, would have a new connotation. It would not be the result of an increase in prices, nor of skimming the income of the consumer, but rather, the result of higher efficiency and productivity of labor and management.

In the present situation, where increased rewards and even increased profits depend on the possibility of increasing prices and not solely on increased efficiency, the efficiency is of no concern to the employees. Rather, it is their concern only in a negative sense. If the profit is taken away by corporate income tax, it is not the business enterprise who suffers; the growth of these enterprises into giants is the best proof of this. It is the consumer and the employees who suffer under the concept of corporate taxes, as these taxes are projected into the prices which the employees, in their function as consumers, have to repay.

Conventional taxation removes that part of the profit which should be shared by those who contribute to produce it. The profit of any enterprise can be divided into two parts —one which goes toward investment, the other which is divided among those who, as employees, made the profit possible.

Profit sharing is meaningful only under conditions of stable prices; this means that profits should be the result of higher productivity by labor. Profit sharing would provoke a permanent pressure by the employees toward a greater efficiency of the economic performance of any enterprise. In practice this means first of all a higher level of managerial skill. The higher degree of productivity, of course, meets the expectation of the employee as it increases the size of the "pie" to be divided.

Under our present economic system, in which profits are not always determined by a higher productivity of labor, we face a tremendous contradiction in terms. Enterprises that perform efficiently are "punished" since part of their profits are skimmed off through taxation. If profit sharing is involved in these enterprises, the employees suffer from this taxation as well. Less efficient enterprises, where profits are not achieved, are favored to the extent that they can write off their losses. On top of this, as the taxes on their goods are included in the prices, the consumer has to pay the taxes whereas the enterprise can use these payments to cover its losses. Thus inefficient enterprises, instead of being at least economically "punished" for not being more efficient, are rewarded, and those who do fulfill the duties as users of the nation's capital are punished.

Profit sharing (once more, only under conditions of stable prices) could turn out to be a most effective and attractive instrument for creating a new feeling that one is performing a meaningful effort in which both the consumer, i.e., the nation as a whole, and the producer are benefiting.

(It is generally known that profit sharing has succeeded in only about 40% of the relatively few businesses where it has been practiced. The reason for this is that it has been used only as an incentive on the part of management to increase the effort of the workers. Another reason for the small success of profit sharing is that it is being used under conditions of permanent price increases. With stable prices, the worker would not be penalized if, despite his own best efforts, the company's profits did not increase enough to increase his wages. We have a socioeconomic climate in which eroding worker morale is increasing. Unless we make the economy serve man, and unless profit is accrued by serving the consumer, this process of demoralization will continue.)

We should also deal with the problem that may arise if the owner of the business enterprise makes a profit. We should distinguish between profit that remains in the business enterprise or is shared and profit that leaves the enterprise, entering the realm of private and personal income. As long as the profit remains in the enterprise, it belongs to the enterprise and may be open to profit sharing but not to taxation. If the owner takes out as much as the tax-free limit, i.e., remains within the income bracket that is not burdened by social share, he should not pay any share whatsoever. If he takes out more than that, he should pay a social share and contribute to the redistribution of income.

Stabilizing prices and making sure profits and rewards are not the result of consumer exploitation are some of the first preconditions of effective profit sharing. Profit sharing, together with stable prices skimming and the redistribution of income would have an effect on phenomenal scope and dimension, for our economy would not be supporting the privileged, but helping the underprivileged.

STABLE PURCHASING POWER

For the money supply to be used as a real macroeconomic tool, the money must have a stable purchasing power. In the same way that the economy is not able to create the needed money supply from the performance of its markets, it is also, through these mechanisms, unable to secure a stable purchasing power. The "invisible hand" needs to be replaced by the *visible* hand—the macroorgan. As stable purchasing power implicitly means a price level that is stable, it should become the duty of the macroorgan, the government, to secure this level.

We must determine whether this concept of a stable price level should refer to rewards and prices, or only to prices. As rewards are incentives without which no economy can perform efficiently, the implementation of wage and price controls ends up being, more often than not, a simplistic administrative measure that has done and will always do more harm than good. The concept of stable prices must be connected with the notion of growing rewards.

If a stable price level is maintained, increases in salaries and profit would no longer be the result of an increase in prices, but of an increase in the efficiency of the economic performance due to the working effort of all the employees. It is, then, both logical and just to have the profit shared by increasing salaries, which, in turn, would support the initiative to be more efficient. The failure to relate stable prices and increasing rewards proves detrimental to one of the most important elements of economic life—the incentive to perform better.

Stable prices are a matter not only of nominal cost, but of quality. If the price of a commodity remains the same but the quality decreases, the price–value actually changes as well. If prices were stable, the competitive market would force a lowering of the price only in an exceptional case. More often, the impetus would be to reduce the quality— which, in effect, would be to increase the real price. Therefore, we have to create a market which fosters competition of quality.

It is essential for economics to create this new kind of market. The assumption that the market determines prices is a myth that has been perpetrated for decades. It is generally recognized that competition is shifting more and more toward a competition by advertising only—attempts to persuade a consumer to buy one commodity over another. While qualitative competition is not altogether absent, it is, to a frightening degree, pushed into the background. Competition should emphasize the quality of commodities and services, including treatment of the consumer.

In this context, the role of small producers and shops is very important. These small businesses provide alternatives of their own to the buyer. The consumer should have varieties to compare—and the right to choose. For small businesses to survive, they need to be given the chance to become real competitors. This is possible only through the active support of the government. This backing should not be viewed as a subsidizing of these businesses, but as a supporting of the consumer. One possibility is that the rate of skimming could be lowered for small businesses, thus increasing their profit margin and the level of their ability to compete with corporate producers. In addition, such measures as the controlling of imports could be active tools in intensifying competition and lessening the all-pervasive control of big business over our market.

There is another major area to consider when discussing stable prices. According to conventional theories, such as the Phillips Curve, stable prices lead to unemployment. If this is actually the case, then the whole notion of stable prices becomes doubtful. We must be able to guarantee stable prices *with* full employment.

First of all, the credit supply by the government would offer means to achieve full employment. Stable prices could be detrimental to employment if we did not, at the same time, increase the incentive to work. By combining the concept of stable prices with increasing rewards, one of the essential factors in unemployment could be avoided. Increasing rewards—raising purchasing power—would then be tied to increasing productivity, and vice versa. Thus greater supply would meet greater demand.

Furthermore, the rate of skimming would result in a decrease in the price of lower-income consumer expenditures. This would, by its very nature, increase the demand for mass-produced goods. (According to the Bureau of Statistics' *Consumer Expenditures and Incomes 1960–61*, households with incomes after taxes of $15,000 and over spend 77% of their income; those from $10,000 to $14,999 spend 91.7% of their income; and those from $7,500 to $9,999 spend 96.8%. The lower income groups spend all that they earn. This statistical evidence indicates that an increase in income in the higher-income level groups leads only

partly to higher consumption, whereas an increase in the income of the lower-income groups would go toward increased
consumption. We can therefore see that the decisive factor
is not how great the aggregate income is, but how great the
income is of those groups who would use the increase in income as purchasing power and thus meet the growing
supply.)

The effect of introducing a stable price level would also
have far-reaching consequences in the socioeconomic climate. People would feel that the benefit of their working
effort would be radiating into all pores of the economy,
thereby reaching all consumers. They would be living on
solid foundations—they would not be deprived of their savings and the purchasing power of their earnings by inflation.
People would become aware that the economy was geared
toward the interests of the consumer, and that profits were
becoming rewards for increasing the well-being of the nation. Trade unions would concentrate on greater efficiency
as the only source of wage increase, instead of merely
fighting for higher wages which are, in the last analysis, paid
for by the consumer, including those very same members of
the union. All of this is not a question of ideology, a matter
of implementing new regulations, nor a "change in human
nature." It would be, rather, an intellectual and logical response to the creation of a new socioeconomic environment.
Because the law of the jungle now exists in the realm of
prices, everyone is forced to apply it. Once we replace this
jungle with an economy based on civilized values, these
very same people with the very same properties will, by the
fact that they are thinking human beings, act according to
the benefits which this new environment offers them.

We can see that the preconditions of stable prices are not
as simple as current monetary theories suggest—an increase
in the money supply of 4%–5% or a fine tuning between fiscal and monetary policy. Achieving stable prices

requires a whole level of complex measures. We have already suggested some of them. Many special disciplines will have to be developed to study the economy from this perspective in order to choose all the correct measures for guaranteeing a stable price level.

These measures, for example, will have to encompass a means for preventing extraordinary events from disturbing the price level. We have seen to what extent the existing concept of prices allows for economic disaster by the impact of the recent price increases in imported oil—despite the fact that this increase amounted to only 1%–2% of the GNP. (Actually, an increase of $1 in imported oil projects an increase of $5 onto the price of the final product.) The increase in oil and gasoline prices triggered a chain reaction of price rises. But if the principle of stable prices had been in effect, measures would have been introduced that would have either curtailed or avoided this general price increase.

In anticipation of such an event, a contingency fund could have been established which would have absorbed the price increase of imported oil. By absorbing this rise, the resultant price spiral in other areas of the economy could have been avoided. Such a fund could have been created, for instance, by a contribution from the budget or by using a portion of skimmed money as a reserve.

In the area of consumer expenditures, measures aimed at keeping the price level stable could have an effect of phenomenal scope. If we look at consumer unit expenditures (for 1960, as noted by the Bureau of Labor and Statistics) by type of product and service, we find that 76.6% of the income of the $1,000 to $1,999 income group was spent on food and housing expenditures. The amount decreases gradually to 57% of the $6,000 to $7,000 group. What this means is that approximately half of the households in this country spend more than 50% of their income on relatively few items.

We should bear in mind that in stabilizing final prices, we are implicitly fixing the prices of the material and energy involved in the production of the commodities. Establishing a stable price level that does not negatively influence incentive, efficiency, and employment, then, could feasibly affect at least half the populace in terms of purchasing power alone. It is not necessary, though, to fix the prices of all goods. Concentrating on stabilizing the prices of those commodities that are necessities for people (which are, in most cases, the only goods half the population can afford) is sufficient enough as a beginning. For the prices of commodities which are luxuries (such as hand-sewn suits as opposed to machine-sewn ones), it is of no immediate consequence whether the prices are fixed or not.

Whatever means are used to implement the concept of stable prices, they will necessarily involve a complex of measures. But above all, it needs to be stressed that a stable price level should be accepted as a *basic economic principle,* one which is the responsibility of the macroorgan and one which cannot be left to so-called market forces or arbitrary actions. Past experience has demonstrated that stable prices have not been very successful. Part of the failure has been due to their being based on administrative or legislative measures. Furthermore, stable prices were usually connected to stable rewards, thus eliminating incentive. In addition, stable prices have been treated as an isolated problem. Stable prices, like any other basic economic factor, are part of the performance of an integrated economy. We therefore have to connect the principle of stable prices with other far-reaching changes of the economic system, such as the government taking responsibility for the money and credit supply and full employment, abandoning fiscal interference with enterprises, introducing the rate of skimming and social shares, and creating a more competitive market. Viewing the economy as an integrated system is the necessary departure point for achieving stable prices, as well as for other goals.

We can now understand the importance of the government's having an economic tool at its disposal. Such a tool could provide us with the opportunity for controlling our economy and for orienting it toward certain goals. We are consequently faced with an issue we have already touched upon: who should have the power to decide toward what goal and whose interest the economy should be oriented? Can an *economic* democracy give the nation the potential of becoming the master of the fate of its economy?

PART 5

ECONOMIC DEMOCRACY

NEW FRAMES OF REFERENCE FOR ECONOMICS

The most outstanding feature of our contemporary and mature mixed economy is the lack of any goal. It is analogous to a boat without a navigator; although everybody desires to reach a point of destination, nobody knows where the boat may finally land. All of us want to have an economy that is efficient and has full employment and a stable price level, but we are still confronted with the problems of high unemployment, even higher inflation, and a decreasing efficiency of the economy as a whole.

The frame of reference of conventional economics, as we have demonstrated, is not the study of the performance of the system, nor the problem of achieving a goal, but the study of allocation of resources and/or of economic laws. This framework, and the claim that economics, as a science, has to be value-free, eliminates the concept of goals in economics.

Our contemporary means of setting out to attain a goal is accomplished by economists advising the government. Unfortunately, as their theories are not centered around the performance of the economy, but only around isolated components such as allocation, they do not produce a tool that, when applied, can solve any economic problem. Theories which involve a certain increase in money supply or a tuning of fiscal and monetary policies—which are actually trial-and-error approaches—as the means of solving problems such as inflation or unemployment, have to fail. In point of fact, these theories are responsible for the dead end in economics and our inability to resolve the most burning economic problems.*

If economists would study the economic reality—the performance of an integrated system—they would discover that this system is moving in a direction, via forces inherent in the system, toward a goal nobody wants. This leaves us with two alternatives. We can either observe this direction and

* A demonstration of the impotence of conventional economics was given at 1974's summit meeting between President Ford and America's leading economists. Professor Samuelson wrote about the first meeting: ". . . But for once, there was a measure of agreement among twenty of them. Both conservative and liberal economists agreed that the economy will be weak in its growth next year." (*Newsweek,* Sept. 16, 1974) *The New York Times* reported that "a group of the nation's most distinguished economists agreed yesterday by a vote of 21 to 2, that the government should be asked to repeal a number of long standing laws and regulations which, in the view of the majority, impede competition and inefficiency and increase prices." (Sept. 24, 1974) This consensus referred to the repealing of such regulations as those requiring trucks to make return trips empty, even when cargo is available, and to the revoking of laws under which fruits and vegetables are required to be destroyed so that they cannot be sold at cut-rate prices.

There is no doubt that these kinds of measures offend common sense and that they do not demand the sophisticated knowledge of leading economists to be refuted. Still, these recommendations are the only ones that have been accepted by such a majority of economists. If carried out, they would be impotent in resolving a single issue proposed for discussion by this summit meeting. It should therefore not be surprising when Samuelson writes: "The correct message came out of the summit. Fighting inflation will at best be a prolonged and costly affair . . . Not a rosy outlook but a sad truth." (*Newsweek,* Oct. 7, 1974) be satisfied with predictions of the state of the economy within a certain time span, or we can be concerned with the orientation of the system and try to control it. In both cases we face the problem of values. Whether we continue to let unemployment and inflation occur or whether we try to eliminate them, each decision or lack of one is based on values.

Apart from this orientation toward the direction of the system, we are faced with still another orientation, which is also not value-free. The economy represents, among other things, a permanent conflict situation between the interests of the producer (in the widest sense of the word) and the consumer. As the economy and market have grown, the producers have developed into corporations of fantastic dimensions. What started as a perfectly competitive situation has developed into a market that is now very much imperfect, a situation in which the actors in the spheres of production have become far stronger than those in the spheres of consumption. The consumers have become an object of manipulation; their dollar vote has become very much inflated. The producers, being more powerful, are able to gear the whole economic process toward their own interests, while the consumers are unable to change it toward theirs. Remaining neutral in this situation simply supports the status quo.

Economics, therefore, is not as value-free as economists claim it to be. They end up only defining away the most essential aspects of the economy, those aspects which are actually value-laden. With this approach, it is no wonder that the concept of goals falls outside of their frame of reference. If we intend to orient the economy, we must formulate a goal that the system can approach.

We should distinguish here between two types of goals: those which are derived from the essence of the economy as it stands and those which are desired goals. The basic aim of the economy is to serve the consumer. The economy must be, therefore, consumer-oriented. (Generally speaking, when the Western economic system is called a consumer economy, it is meant that the whole economy is geared toward increasing the amount of goods and services to be consumed. This leads the producers to emphasize consumption and motivates them to influence consumers to buy these goods and services. This type of consumer society is, in actuality, enterprise-oriented, for a true consumer-oriented society would stress the interests of the consumer as the basic motivation of the enterprises, and not consumption.)

Orienting the economy toward the consumer encompasses giving the consumer five basic economic rights to which he should always be entitled. The first involves the consumer's inalienable *economic right to influence the performance* of the economy. As the consumer represents practically the whole nation, each citizen should feel that the economy is serving the nation as a whole. The second basic right of the consumer is related to an *efficient economy*. Inefficiency of the economy means that the consumer is deprived of potential income and services. The efficiency of economic performance should be seen as the degree to which the economy is serving the consumer. The greater the degree of efficiency, the more that can be produced with the same or smaller input. This benefits the consumer in that it increases the availability of working power and material. Efficiency also provides for shorter working hours, less strain, social security, education—in general, the quality of life can be improved on the basis of higher competency in the working process.

Full employment, the third basic right, is a part of this efficiency. Since it makes full use of the available working capacity, full employment means that the citizen's right to work is protected. Fourth, a *stable price level* protects the citizen against being deprived of the purchasing power of his earnings by inflation, however small its rate may be. Finally, the given economic system has proven itself unable to deal with problems of the ecology. The problems of air and water pollution and of the growing scarcity of resources, especially of raw materials, cannot be solved by thinking of input and output only in terms of price units. *Ecological equilibrium* is essential. Stable prices, full employment, an efficiently performing economy, the ability of the consumer to influence this economy, and ecological equilibrium are the *inalienable economic rights* of every citizen, the core of humanomics. Without these rights, the notion of inalienable human rights is meaningless.

The other type of goal, the desired one, should be derived from the democratic right of the citizen. It is whatever the citizen wants the economy to be aimed toward. The concern of the citizen for a just distribution of income, health services, a decent quality of life, etc., would all lead to the formulation of desired goals. These types of goals can be expressed within the framework of democracy and can be implemented by the existing democratic mechanism. But the essentials have to be seen as the foundation on which the whole economy should be based.

In mixed economies, only one of these fundamentals has been achieved. Business enterprises have reached a remarkable level of efficiency. Management itself is applying a science dealing specifically with management. Yet the other goals of the macroorgan have not been attained. The government does not have a discipline that contains the frames of reference for advising it on how to achieve these essential goals.

From the viewpoint of full employment and a stable price level alone, the Soviet model may be superior to the Western one. But, on the other hand, the Soviet model did not achieve an efficient performance on the enterprise level. We tried to explain the reasons for this in the chapter on planning. As far as the rights of the consumer are concerned, their economy is geared toward the political motives of the "owners" of the means of production, the party leadership. Consequently, the consumer is deprived even of the limited rights experienced in the Western model. Efficiency on the enterprise level means, of necessity, going beyond simply employing everyone who is willing to work. The prices are inflated even though their level may be stable. Real wages cover far less than in the West.

The Soviet model proves that it is not a great economic problem to achieve full employment and stable prices. Both can be achieved merely by administrative measures. The real difficulty lies in basing these imperatives on efficient economic performance. While the Western model has attained efficiency in the microsphere, the enterprises and the economy as a whole will decline to the Soviet level if unemployment and inflation continue to prevail and affect the functioning of business.

In the Soviet model, efficiency is measured by the fulfillment of target figures. The Western model measures it by the profit or the profit rate. We should be able to view efficiency with a different perspective: the efficiency of *the whole economic performance,* of which enterprise competency is one component.

In this context, efficiency is measured by the degree to which the capacities of the economy are being utilized and, in addition, by how well the economy is able to cope with other problems, such as ecology and the quality of life. This involves, for example, a great deal more economizing of raw materials and the necessity of using more materials that are not so scarce, even if it is at higher costs.

This concept of efficiency has to be understood in a completely different way from that of the classical and conventional approach. Recycling and making use of solar energy and the wealth of the oceans are beyond the scope of efficiency of the enterprise level and must be seen in the context of the performance of the economy as a whole. While, for example, the most efficient way for an enterprise to produce may necessitate polluting, this is not without its social cost. The role of the macroorgan in securing efficiency of the whole economic process must be a new central point of concern.

A popular explanation for why the economy's essential goals have not been achieved is that "vested interests" stand in the way. While these interests may play their role, the basic obstacle is that economics is not viewed as the study of the performance of the economy as an integrated system of thinking human beings. Economists will have to be more concerned with studying past performance, not in order to predict the future, but to be able to change the present.

This study of the "physiology" of the economic system should not be an end in itself. It should be aimed at discovering the causes of "pathological" phenomena such as unemployment, inflation, and the extent to which the system is oriented against the interests of the consumer.

It should not be confined to answering "how the economy performed," but should be geared toward positing the question of *how to orient the economic performance toward a goal we want to achieve*. The task behind this question will advise us how to orient our economy and help us understand the causes of and the cures for our malaise. Economics should thus become the tool enabling us to control the motion of our economic system and to "navigate the boat."

Although these frames of reference may seem revolutionary, they are by no means new. Adam Smith himself suggested a political economy that would be a science of the statesman, with the object of providing plentiful revenue or subsistence for the people.

The task confronting today's politician goes far beyond providing plentiful revenue, although even the most affluent societies have not yet fully actualized this task since the time Smith first expressed it. While the problem of an abundant subsistence could hardly have been solved then, the problems of full employment and stable purchasing power were not issues during Smith's lifetime, nor were problems of the environment, of a competitive market, or of a shortage of raw materials and energy.

The science of economy has to become the intellectual tool of the government. The development of economics went astray and lost itself in irrelevant issues and artificial problems. It is necessary to return to those frames of reference that were once at the cradle of the science of economy.

THE GOAL

The essential goals of any mature economy are full employment, stable purchasing power, the efficiency of economic performance, and the orientation of the economy toward the interests of the consumer. These components actually should be regarded as one economic goal, as none of them can be isolated and solved as a single issue. We should repeat, furthermore, that any desired goals must be based on these essentials. Otherwise, we are undermining the foundations on which the economy is based.

In order to create an economy that is oriented toward certain goals, be they essential or desired, there must be a subjective will and desire to achieve them. Even though the essential goals may be accepted by the overwhelming majority of the nation, of economists, and of politicians, this consensus alone is not a sufficient precondition for the creation of a goal-oriented economy. There are three additional preconditions to be met.

The *first condition* is the establishment of an *economic*

macroorgan. This means that there must be a macroorgan—for all practical purposes, the government—which is entrusted with the task of taking all necessary measures to achieve the goals. Mixed economies do not have such a macroorgan. The government is a political organ acting under political considerations. A mature society is an integrated system of which the governmental apparatus is but one of its subsystems, however, both theoretically and in practice, the modern government is seen and acts as an organ external to the economy.

The government has expenditures and expects the nation to "pay its bills"; the budget is constructed on political considerations and is projected into the economy in the form of taxes. Only when economic problems are political issues does the government step into the picture, and, even then, it intervenes like a careless fireman, often doing more damage in trying to extinguish the fire than the fire itself would do. Although the government accepts the philosophy of free enterprise, its approach interferes with the freedom of individual enterprises. It introduces taxes which deprive the economy of the necessary means for performing efficiently. The government taxes partly because the nation should "pay its bills" and partly in order to avoid "overheating" the economy—meaning that the economy should not fully utilize its capacity, as such a state of affairs could foster inflation.

The ludicrous role the government plays in the economy is typified in its approach to employment. It is ironic that we are confronted with the problem of unemployment in a period in which there are tremendous needs to be met which require the full working potential of the nation. In the future we will be facing far greater needs for labor, both manual and mental, as the conservation of raw material and energy creates new industries connected with recycling and the production of new sources of energy and raw material. Labor saving machines will not be sufficient to cover the subsequently expanding need for more labor. Making use of all the available labor, then, will be a consideration of the first order.

Instead of viewing unused labor as a potential force to be utilized and one which could solve many of the dilemmas of the most advanced countries, unemployment has become an enigma and an aggravation both for the individual and for the society. We can only conclude that there must be something wrong with the theories and the system on which they are based if society is forced to treat unemployment as a bane and cannot make use of this most natural source of wealth.

At present, the first consideration of the government is not full or meaningful employment, a political concern, but what should it do with the unemployed? The government will spend money for benefits (France now compensates 90% wages to its unemployed for a whole year) or for any type of work, even economically unimportant jobs, in order to fight the social and political consequences of unemployment. Thus the citizens, through our present form of taxation, are paying for a lack of work instead of for the result of productive work. The absurdity of this situation lies, of course, not with those who lost the opportunity to work, but with the system that has no organ bearing the total responsibility for full employment.

The government's use of the money supply demonstrates this same political motivation. It tightens the money supply in order to avoid the inflationary effect of an "overheated economy," but what it is actually doing is preventing the economy from working up to its full capacity. Unemployment thus increases a politically undesirable problem. To diminish the number of unemployed, then, the government increases the money supply and perhaps lowers taxes. But this only fosters inflation.

The government thus assumes a role of trade-off, balancing between full employment and stable prices so that neither becomes an extreme that could have political repercussions. The possibility of having an economy with both full employment and stable prices is not considered as a viable possibility in theory or in practice.

The philosophical foundation of mixed economies does not consider the need for an economic macroorgan, one which is responsible for the realization of certain goals. The only economic goals conceived of in this philosophy are microeconomic ones, i.e., profit. Even if this responsibility is stated by law (such as the Labor Act of 1946), its expression remains a political imperative. It has not changed the role of the government.

If we do not believe that the economy needs to be goal-oriented, there is obviously no reason to create an organ for this task. We are then leaving everything to the "market forces"; the goals of the enterprises will dominate, and the economy will remain a boat without a navigator. The result can only be some form of chaos.

At a final glance, there may seem to be a similarity between our proposed model and that of a planned economy. The decisive difference, however, lies in the concepts of goals and the role of the macroorgan. The planned economy can be pictured as one giant enterprise run by the planning center. This center, the government (or, more accurately, the politburo), is at the same time the macro- and the microorgan. It acts as manager of all enterprises and as a government at the same time. Target figures determine what has to be produced, the prices, the wages, the number of employees, the money supply, the credit policy, and what has to be consumed, to name just a few areas within its scope.

In our proposed model, the government must not take measures that command and interfere with the efficient performance of the business enterprise. At the same time, though, the government has to be concerned with the efficient performance of the system as a whole and with giving the consumer a strong position in the market. This role of the macroorgan determines the tools it has to have at its disposal.

The *macroeconomic tools* of the government are consequently the *second precondition* of a goal-oriented economy. These tools, such as the money and credit supply, provide the government with the means of orienting the economy toward greater efficiency and the interests of the consumer.

It is not sufficient, however, to have just a macroorgan and tools at its disposal. The decisive element is how to use these tools. It is this "know-how," in the end, that will determine whether we achieve our goals. Surgical equipment, for example, is only a precondition for the surgeon. He can only use these tools with a knowledge of medicine as "scientific advice" and with an ability to apply this advice. In the same way, without scientific guidance as to how to make necessary use of the tools of the macroorgan, we will never achieve our goals.

Thus, the *third precondition* is establishing a means for *comprehensive economic advising*. This counseling would be based on a concrete formulation of economic goals and a way of achieving them in a program of action. The program would involve the application of the findings of a scientific discipline whose frames of reference would be the study of the performance of the system.

A program of full employment, for example, would be based on a study of the sources of existing or expected unemployment. Furthermore, if there were people unemployed due to their lacking skill, the program would deal with the problem not only of employing them, but of helping them gain skill as well. In areas where there were skilled people without work, the program would create the means for employing them.

These studies would have to encompass the optimal utilization of working capacity from two angles. The first would be a horizontal one, including industrial centers, counties, and states. The second approach would be vertical, involving branches of industries. Existing trends, future directions, interactions and interdependencies between regions and between branches of industries would also be included in the analyses. In other words, these studies would be a sort of "anatomy and physiology" of the regions and branches of the economy.

A program for stable prices would also be based on an analysis of the needed money supply in all areas of the economy as a whole. Earmarked money would only be a small proportion of the total money supply (10%–20%). Therefore, the major portion of the money supply would be accessible to businesses through normal channels. Earmarked money, first of all, would be available only if the enterprises themselves did not have the necessary means for financing projects. It is quite conceivable that the capital market could provide all the money needed for investments, in which case assigned deposits by the government would not be needed.

Above all, the studies and programs of action will have to take into consideration that it should remain the autonomous decision of the individual enterprises as to how they should act. To repeat, the task of the macroorgan is not to create full employment, but, by its use of the money supply and other macroeconomic tools, to *create conditions conducive to full employment.*

Thus, the primary task of these programs involves knowing the working of the economy in the same way that the doctor must know the physiology of the human body. But while the physician cannot change the anatomy and physiology of the body, we should realize that the economy, as a system of thinking human beings, is always changing both its "anatomy" and its "physiology," and that it is in our power to control these changes and to orient them in a desired direction.

If we concentrate on just the essential goals, we would find ourselves not needing large amounts of data. We would have to know the overall needed money and credit supply and the proportion to be earmarked. We would have to take into account the means of introducing a perfect price control mechanism and a truly competitive market. In addition, we would have to consider how great the rate of skimming should be, and the breakdown of its rate for redistributing income on the one hand and influencing the power of the consumer on the other. These tools would not only provide the means for directing the economy toward full employment, but they would also actualize a most desired and profound change in the orientation of the whole system.

However important the basic goals are, if the issues confronting the mature economy remain unresolved, they will lead and are leading toward a deep economic and social crisis. Finding new sources of energy and raw material, improving our environment, and coping with a host of other difficult areas are problems that cannot be solved by enterprises or by granting money for research alone. As we have shown, isolated treatment of these issues could create more dangerous complications. A program which advises the government on how to deal with these problems requires a very thorough study of the performance of the economy as a whole and of the whole social system, of which the economy is only a subsystem.

Such a comprehensive program is undertaken in planned economies, but they do not take into consideration that the economy is a system of thinking human beings. Without using a methodology derived from this perspective, plans will be counterproductive, and goals will never be achieved. Our proposed model would use the study as a basis for programs that would explain how to utilize the macrotools in a way that would not be restricting on the freedom of the enterprises. The study would entail modes of implementing desired goals on the basis of essential goals. It would describe the stages of realization of the program and provide the means for making technology serve man. These are the real frames of reference for our times.

Two questions now arise: First, can such important and basic changes, both in thinking and in practice, be brought about before our social and economic crises deepen further? The answer is yes. Once we accept the basic assumption that our economy is a system *sui generis* which needs a macroorgan and macrotools, we can immediately take initial steps that will at least slow down the trend toward higher unemployment and inflation.

The government would first have to control prices, not necessarily all, but at least those which affect the market basket of the majority of the nation. The social share would have to be introduced, not for normal budgetary expenditures, but directly toward stated objectives, with the purpose of redistributing income. The rate of skimming would be used, at least in part, for redistributing income by decreasing the prices of commodities in the lower income groups' market basket and by increasing it in the higher income groups. To reverse the increasing trend of unemployment, the government would not apply the useless measures of fiscal and monetary tuning. It would start by depositing funds in the banks earmarked for areas of the economy functioning at low capacity. The construction industry, for instance, in its present crisis, would have access to credit at very low interest rates. The same would apply for mass transportation and for productive working opportunities for the young and especially for minorities.

The second question is: Although we may start to build an economic science, already tragically late, will the creation of this science be any guarantee of its being accepted as a guide and implemented as a means of achieving our goals? The answer again is yes. The reason is economic democracy.

ECONOMIC DEMOCRACY

In 1946 Congress declared it the responsibility of the federal government to promote maximum employment, production, and purchasing power. Seldom has any legislative act expressed to such a degree the political will of the whole nation. In this respect the Employment Act can be seen as a triumph of democracy.

Still, more than a quarter of a century later, we are faced with an inflation rate of over 10% and a growing rate of unemployment, forecast to be 9% or more, as well as millions of people employed only part-time. These figures do not even include those who were looking for jobs in vain for so long that they dropped out of the labor market, nor do they account for people who did not find meaningful jobs.

Full employment, as we have said, is more than just a desire of the whole nation; it is a democratic right. But what is the meaning of a citizen's democratic rights if such relatively modest goals of full employment and stable prices are beyond the reach of the government? We are confronted with a great tragedy of democracy. Citizens have democratic rights, but, in the area of the economy, they are denied them.

In politics, majority decisions are carried out by the government. But as far as the economy is concerned, the government is not able to act according to the wishes of the populace, even if it wants to do so. While political decisions and the exertion of political rights rarely, if ever, affect the daily lives of citizens, economic phenomena, such as unemployment and inflation, have an impact on them every day. They determine the conditions in households as well as those in the working environment. Still, the citizens and the government are helpless—the belief and faith in democracy is fading away.

We have already mentioned how the inability to solve unemployment in the thirties undermined democracy in Europe. The desire to have a government in command of the economy, one which would offer full employment, led to fascism. We are now experiencing a crisis involving the same basic economic phenomena, but the political reaction to the situation is yet to be seen. While it is unlikely that the response will be the same as it was in the thirties, it may be even more dramatic and tragic unless we are able to turn the economy toward the interests of man. The possibility of democracy being pushed aside for the sake of achieving full employment and stable prices is not a remote one.

If we look back, for a moment, at the cradle of democracy —the *polis* in the city-state of ancient Greece—we find an *active democracy*. Citizens were not supposed to lead just private lives; political participation was a way of life. (The word "idiot" is of Greek origin and referred to people who were not active citizens.) Citizenship was associated with taking part in various functions, in cult ceremonies, in the military service, and in the legislature. Democracy was by no means merely the election of representatives of the people.

Today, however, democracy is reduced to simply electing representatives—it is not active but defensive. Its main purpose is to protect the private citizen from the overwhelming power of the government. The role played by the representatives is basically one of limiting the government for the sake of the individual freedom of its people.

If we want to extend political democracy into economic democracy, we will find that we have to think in terms of different premises. The economy is the result of the activity of the whole working population. The citizens of the *polis*, who participated in the political life of their city-state, provided the basis for their active democracy. The working citizen in our society, similarly, since he is an active economic agent, should enjoy the same rights in the realm of economics that he has in that of politics.

As far as the sociopolitical life of the nation is concerned, the government has the benefit of a very high intellectual level on which it can operate. The Constitution, our system of laws and regulations, and the studies and research which exist in all areas of sociopolitical life are an apparatus which enables the government to act according to the wishes of its population. (If this is by far not always the case, it is because powerful interests prevent such possibilities from materializing and because the nation lacks an economic macroorgan to act on its behalf.) Thus, if the nation declares its desires for the realization of human rights in political terms, the government has the means to implement and enforce this imperative. If the nation declares its desire for *economic* human rights, however, the government is at a loss. It has neither the intellectual nor the operative tools to fulfill this task. There is no economic discipline that studies the performance of the economic system as a whole.

Actually, democracies have only half a government. It can represent the nation well only as far as sociopolitical problems are concerned. The other half, in the realm of the economy, is not seen as the responsibility of the government. Other forces determine the orientation of the performance of the system. They are so powerful that they can even interfere with the political will of the majority of the nation.

We take for granted the intellectual level on which the government operates. Throughout the course of many generations, we have had political scientists, social scientists, universities, and research institutes at our disposal. Without these intellectual tools, the mature society would have absolute chaos. We could not have courts without jurisprudence; we could not have a civilized society without a consistent system of laws. Even such a simple problem as traffic regulations must be based on expertise and an operative apparatus.

Unfortunately, we also take it for granted that our economy does *not* have the intellectual or operative tools needed to meet the goals of the democratic will of the nation. Therefore, in order to have an economy with full employment and a stable price level, it is not sufficient to accept an Employment Act. As a matter of fact, the acceptance of this act was deceptive and has created illusions, despite the honest motivations which may have existed at its inception.

Our analysis of a modern economy has thus far led us to the following conclusions:

1) The production of any product is the result of the working effort of practically all the professions in a nation. In this sense, it should be seen as a *product of the nation*.
2) Any owner of a business enterprise, apart from making use of his own capital investment, uses part of the nation's material and cultural wealth. This kind of "joint tenancy" requires a macroorgan to be responsible for guaranteeing that the "capital" of the nation is treated *in the interest of the nation*.
3) Production based on applied science has the faculty of

lucroactivity, i.e., of radiating "gain" that is inherently social. This necessitates a macroorgan whose duty it is to care for this potential *wealth of the nation* and to optimize the effect of the lucroactivity.

4) The economy is a system of thinking human beings, an organically integrated system, possessing in its dynamism the orientation of the system itself. The present orientation is essentially geared toward the interests of the business enterprise. To orient the economy toward the *interests of the nation*—in economic terms, the consumer—there must be a macroorgan to formulate the interests of the nation into a *concrete goal* and to implement measures that would gear the economy toward this goal.

5) The nation, being both the producer and the consumer, the owner of joint tenancy and of the social "gain," must have the *right to approve* such goals and the means of their realization.

Thus, the right of the nation to control its economy—which is the content of the concept of economic democracy—is not only a political imperative, but is the rational conclusion to draw from the analysis of a mature economy.

We can envision, then, a whole process being initiated by starting toward goals, no matter how limited they may be, and by the government's assuming the responsibility for bringing about the changes in the system necessary to gear the system toward these goals. Economic goals in programs may become controversial because they will affect various interests within the nation. It is for this particular reason that economic programs could, and should, become election issues. In the course of this process, we can also expect that real economic democracy would evolve.

The logical consequence of goals being embodied in economic proposals is for political parties to adapt them into their platforms. Their platforms would then offer to the citizens not just political stands, which are usually ambiguous by their nature, but *concrete* economic programs. These plans of action would express the few most important items in the budget—what the parties expect to accomplish in such fields as education, health, social security, and defense, and the cost of these endeavors, meaning the budget. The budget should not result from trade-offs in allocating money to different departments. It should be, if economic democracy is to have any meaning at all, a binding promise, a kind of socioeconomic contract.

The proposal would formulate what the government would have to fulfill. In electing representatives, the constituency would be accepting the foremost items of the tasks to be fulfilled as well as their cost. This means that the program would also have to entail what the rate of skimming would be, how it would be distributed between groups of consumers, how the social share would be structured and for what purposes it would be used, the areas to benefit from earmarked deposits, the measures to be taken for environmental protection and for securing full employment, and other goals which would include the complex measures to be undertaken and the costs involved in them.

In order for such programs to be meaningful for the layman, they would have to be expressed in terms and in volume so as to be understandable to him. At the same time, the detailed program would be available for evaluation by experts in different fields.

Introducing these economic programs into the political aspect of democracies would mean far more than an expansion of democratic rights into the realm of economy. The fact that concrete programs can be easily checked, as they are expressed in figures, would add a dimension to democratic participation. Proposals would exist not only to catch votes, but to be fulfilled. The fact that the program is binding would, hopefully, eliminate the space for the privilege of powerful corporations. The citizens would feel that they, the creators of the nation's wealth, had a say in the direction of its use.

We can see, just from the effects of taking the first step toward a goal, that economic science would not come about out of a decision to create it. We cannot simply say that we have found new frames of reference and then derive a science with theories, methodology, and epistemology based on this perspective. Economic science will emerge and develop in the process of undertaking the tasks of solving economic problems. Economic theories and methodology will therefore not be based on abstract, definitional statements. They will be derived from the continuing study of the performance of the system, which implicitly means they will be based on economic reality. Just as the physician can cure only by continuing to develop his knowledge of medicine, so can economic goals be achieved only by studying the economic reality.

A picture of a perfect society and economy is not implied here. A society without conflicts, without some degree of injustice, without reflections of the limitations of human beings will never exist. Nor are we inferring that a dramatic change in human nature will occur. What we can achieve with humanomics is the orientation of the society and the economy toward more human goals instead of, as now exists, their heading farther and farther away from humane ends.

We must emphasize that the orientation of the society and the economy toward a goal does not mean that their achievement is a final state, as the content of the goals are part of a changing process. By orientation, we mean that we are approaching a goal, and that we are, hopefully, doing it in an asymptotic way. We will always have to fight to project humane values into the goals and the system. But at least we will have created a system which responds to humane values.

AFTERWORD

America has proven to be the country whose genius was most triggered by the great possibilities offered to mankind by applied science. By applying science to production and to management, the American corporation has become a most efficient transformer of natural wealth and natural forces into productive wealth and energy.

These great historical achievements have had a tremendous impact on the whole world. They have created the socioeconomic revolution of our age. It is not an overstatement to say that no other country in the world has achieved the level that is now a basic characteristic of America.

Yet, on the other hand, America has not been able to create a system which turns these fantastic achievements toward the interests of man. Just the reverse, the United States has become preoccupied with the material side of this great revolution. Human interests have been regarded as secondary, or have not been taken into consideration at all.

The theories on which the American economy is based, as well as all the others, both in the West and in the East, remain deeply enrooted in the past century. They assume that technology will solve the problems of man. It is this tragic shortcoming that undermines the achievements and their impact both in the United States and the world at large.

Just as it has become the great historical role of America to create the immense potentialities of our century, it is also her great historical mission to turn these possibilities into reality. As it is not likely that any other country can fulfill this mission, the future of the world depends to a dramatic degree on whether America can meet this challenge.

I am fully aware that I have touched on only some basic assumptions. I also recognize that once this new science of humanomics emerges, it will develop measures far beyond those mentioned in this book.

The aim of this study has not at all been to offer *the* solution, nor to attempt any kind of blueprint for society. The purpose of this book is to contribute to a discussion of positive solutions to our problems, as opposed to the inflation of doomsday prophesies. The basic assumption that the economy is an integrated system of thinking human beings, that our intellectual ability created this system, and that we should be able to control and not have to predict the future is not too difficult to prove. Yet the issue is not to acknowledge this assumption, but to build on it the principle of the science of economy which will help us to become the conscientious creator of our future.

About the Author

"Humanomics" was born in a Czech prison. In 1949, during the notorious Slansky trials, EUGEN LOEBL, then Czech First Minister of Foreign Trade, was sentenced to life imprisonment by the Soviet government for "treason"—he refused to stop trading with the West. He remained there for eleven years—harassed, sometimes tortured, much of the time in solitary. He had much time to think and slowly came to an agonizing reappraisal both of his beloved Marxism and of capitalism. The result was "humanomics."

In 1960, Loebl was released and allowed to become a common laborer; in 1963, he was "rehabilitated" and appointed Director of the State Bank. In May 1968, Alexander Dubček invested him with the Order of Labor, and preparations were underway for him to join the Dubček government—when Czechoslovakia was invaded by the Soviet Union. Loebl fled to Austria, and then to the United States, where he is now Professor of Economics and Political Science at Vassar College. His articles and books, including *Conversations with the Bewildered* and *Stalinism in Prague,* have appeared all over the world and have been translated into many languages, and he has lectured widely on the problems of economic planning.

Eugen Loebl was born in 1907, and before becoming First Deputy Minister of Foreign Trade, served as the Director of the UNRRA Office in Prague and as a member of the Praesidium of the Economic Committee of the Communist Party of Czechoslovakia. His account of his prison experiences will appear in the fall of 1976. He now lives in New York City.